Home-Style COOKING
~ WITH CREAM SOUP ~

Taste of Home
B O O K S

REIMAN MEDIA GROUP, INC. • GREENDALE, WISCONSIN

Taste of Home

A TASTE OF HOME/READER'S DIGEST BOOK

EDITOR: Janet Briggs
ART DIRECTOR: Nathan Chow
SENIOR LAYOUT DESIGNER: Julie Wagner
PROOFREADER: Linne Bruskewitz
EDITORIAL ASSISTANT: Barb Czysz
RECIPE TESTING AND EDITING: Taste of Home Test Kitchen
FOOD PHOTOGRAPHY: Reiman Photo Studio
COVER PHOTO: Lori Foy

SENIOR EDITOR, RETAIL BOOKS: Jennifer Olski
EXECUTIVE EDITOR, BOOKS: Heidi Reuter Lloyd
CREATIVE DIRECTOR: Ardyth Cope
SENIOR VICE PRESIDENT/EDITOR IN CHIEF: Catherine Cassidy
PRESIDENT: Barbara Newton
FOUNDER: Roy Reiman

Pictured on front cover: Chicken in Creamy Gravy, page 126.
Insert photos on front cover from left to right:
Ham Mushroom Pie, page 35; Quick Mushroom Stew, page 50
and Skillet Enchiladas, page 44.

Pictured on the back cover: Veggie Meatball Medley, page 43.

International Standard Book Number: 0-89821-514-5
Library of Congress Control Number: 2006928039

For other Taste of Home books and products,
visit www.tasteofhome.com.
For more Reader's Digest products and information, visit
www.rd.com (in the United States)
www.rd.ca (in Canada).

Printed in China 1 3 5 7 9 10 8 6 4 2

Carrot Chowder, page 13

CONTENTS

SNACKS

Tomato-Broccoli Chicken Bites (pictured left)

MARTY KINGERY, POINT PLEASANT, WEST VIRGINIA

PREP: 15 min. **BAKE:** 25 min.

2 1/2	cups diced cooked chicken breast
1	can (10 3/4 ounces) reduced-fat reduced-sodium condensed cream of chicken soup, undiluted
1	cup frozen chopped broccoli, thawed and drained
2	small plum tomatoes, seeded and chopped
1	small carrot, grated
1	tablespoon Dijon mustard
1	garlic clove, minced
1/4	teaspoon pepper
1	sheet frozen puff pastry, thawed
1/4	cup grated Parmesan cheese

In a large bowl, combine the first eight ingredients; set aside. On a lightly floured surface, roll pastry into a 12-in. x 9-in. rectangle. Cut lengthwise into four strips and widthwise into three strips. Gently press puff pastry squares into muffin cups coated with nonstick cooking spray.

Spoon chicken mixture into pastry cups. Sprinkle with Parmesan cheese. Bake at 375° for 25-30 minutes or until golden brown. Serve warm.

YIELD: 1 dozen.

Turkey Crescents

MARYE JO TIMMONS, ALEXANDRIA, VIRGINIA

PREP/TOTAL TIME: 30 min.

1/2	cup finely chopped celery
1/4	cup finely chopped onion
1	teaspoon butter
2	cups finely chopped cooked turkey
1	can (10 3/4 ounces) condensed cream of mushroom soup, undiluted
3	packages (8 ounces *each*) refrigerated crescent rolls
	Dill weed

In a nonstick skillet, saute celery and onion in butter for 3-4 minutes or until tender. Add turkey and soup; mix well. Remove from the heat.

Separate crescent dough into 24 triangles. Place 1 tablespoon turkey mixture on the wide end of each triangle; roll up from wide end. Place pointed side down 2 in. apart on greased baking sheets. Curve ends to form crescent shape. Sprinkle with dill. Bake at 350° for 8-9 minutes or until golden brown. Serve immediately.

YIELD: 2 dozen.

In a small microwave-safe bowl, sprinkle gelatin over water; let stand for 1 minute. Microwave on high for 40 seconds; stir. Let stand for 2 minutes or until gelatin is completely dissolved. Stir the gelatin mixture, celery, mayonnaise, lemon juice and onions into soup mixture. Fold in shrimp.

Pour into a 5-cup ring mold coated with nonstick cooking spray. Cover and refrigerate for 8 hours or until set. Invert onto a serving plate. Fill center with lettuce and shrimp if desired. Serve with crackers.

YIELD: 4 1/4 cups.

EDITOR'S NOTE: Reduced-fat or fat-free mayonnaise is not recommended for this recipe.

MOLDED SHRIMP SPREAD

MRS. AUSTIN LOCKE, PRINEVILLE, OREGON

PREP: 15 min. + chilling

- 1   can (10 3/4 ounces) condensed cream of mushroom soup, undiluted
- 1   package (8 ounces) cream cheese, cubed
- 1   envelope unflavored gelatin
- 3   tablespoons cold water
- 1   cup finely chopped celery
- 1   cup mayonnaise
- 3   tablespoons lemon juice
- 4   green onions, finely chopped
- 1/2   pound cooked shrimp, peeled, deveined and coarsely chopped
  Lettuce leaves and additional shrimp, optional
  Assorted crackers

In a saucepan, heat soup and cream cheese over medium heat until cheese is melted, stirring frequently. Remove from the heat; set aside to cool.

SOUPER JOES

ERLENE CORNELIUS, SPRING CITY, TENNESSEE

PREP/TOTAL TIME: 15 min.

- 1   pound ground beef
- 1   can (10 3/4 ounces) condensed cream of mushroom soup, undiluted
- 1   tablespoon onion soup mix
- 1   cup (4 ounces) shredded cheddar cheese
- 8   hamburger buns, split

In a saucepan, cook beef over medium heat until no longer pink; drain. Stir in soup and soup mix; heat through. Add cheese, stirring until melted. Place about 1/3 cupful on each bun.

YIELD: 8 servings.

POPPY SEED SQUARES

JO BADEN, INDEPENDENCE, KANSAS

PREP: 35 min. **BAKE:** 25 min.

1	pound ground beef
1½	cups finely chopped fresh mushrooms
1	medium onion, finely chopped
1	can (10 ¾ ounces) condensed cream of celery soup, *or* mushroom soup, undiluted
1	tablespoon prepared horseradish
1	teaspoon salt
½	teaspoon pepper

CRUST:

3	cups all-purpose flour
2	tablespoons poppy seeds
¾	teaspoon baking powder
¾	teaspoon salt
1	cup shortening
½	cup cold water

In a skillet, cook the beef, mushrooms and onion over medium heat until meat is no longer pink; drain. Add the soup, horseradish, salt and pepper; mix well. Remove from the heat; set aside.

In a bowl, combine the flour, poppy seeds, baking powder and salt. Cut in shortening until the mixture resembles coarse crumbs. Gradually add water, tossing with a fork until a ball forms. Divide dough in half. Roll out one portion into a 15-in. x 10-in. rectangle; transfer to an ungreased 15-in. x 10-in. x 1-in. baking pan.

Spoon meat mixture over dough. Roll out the remaining dough into 15-in. x 10-in. rectangle; place over filling. Bake at 425° for 25 minutes or until golden brown. Cut into small squares.

YIELD: about 10 dozen.

TURKEY TURNOVERS

JULIE WAGNER, NOVI, MICHIGAN

PREP: 15 min. **BAKE:** 30 min.

1	package (3 ounces) cream cheese, softened
1	tablespoon milk
1/2	cup cubed cooked turkey
1/2	cup cooked peas *or* vegetable of your choice
4	teaspoons sliced almonds
1	tablespoon minced fresh parsley
1	tablespoon finely chopped onion
1 1/2	teaspoons diced pimientos
	Dash *each* salt, pepper and garlic powder
1	cup biscuit/baking mix
1/4	cup cold water
1	tablespoon butter, melted
1/2	to 3/4 cup condensed cream of chicken soup, undiluted *or* chicken gravy

In a mixing bowl, beat cream cheese and milk until smooth. Stir in the turkey, peas, almonds, parsley, onion, pimientos, salt, pepper and garlic powder; set aside.

In a bowl, combine biscuit mix and water until a soft dough forms. On a floured surface, knead gently 5-6 times or until dough is no longer sticky. Gently roll into an 11-in. x 7-in. rectangle; cut in half. Spoon half of the turkey mixture onto each. Carefully fold pastry over filling; seal edges tightly with a fork. Brush tops with butter.

Place on a greased baking sheet. Bake at 350° for 30-35 minutes or until golden brown. Meanwhile, heat soup; serve with turnovers.

YIELD: 2 servings.

CHEESY SAUSAGE DIP

CURTIS COLE, DALLAS, TEXAS

PREP/TOTAL TIME: 20 min.

- 1 pound ground beef
- 1 pound bulk pork sausage
- 2 tablespoons all-purpose flour
- 1 can (10 $\frac{3}{4}$ ounces) condensed cream of mushroom soup, undiluted
- 1 can (10 ounces) diced tomatoes and green chilies, undrained
- 1 medium onion, chopped
- 1 tablespoon garlic powder
- 2 pounds process American cheese, cubed

  Tortilla chips

In a large saucepan, cook beef and sausage over medium heat until no longer pink; drain. Sprinkle with flour. Add the soup, tomatoes, onion and garlic powder; mix well.

Bring to a boil; cook and stir for 2 minutes or until thickened. Reduce heat. Add cheese, stirring until melted. Serve warm with tortilla chips. Refrigerate any leftovers.

YIELD: 8 cups.

SPINACH FETA SQUARES

CHRISTINE HALANDRAS, MEEKER, COLORADO

PREP: 10 min. BAKE: 45 min.

- 1 large onion, chopped
- 3 tablespoons butter
- 2 packages (10 ounces *each*) frozen chopped spinach, thawed and squeezed dry
- 1 can (10 $\frac{3}{4}$ ounces) condensed cream of mushroom soup, undiluted
- 4 eggs, beaten
- 1 cup sliced fresh mushrooms
- $\frac{1}{4}$ cup dried bread crumbs
- $\frac{1}{4}$ cup crumbled feta cheese
- $\frac{1}{8}$ teaspoon dried oregano
- $\frac{1}{8}$ teaspoon dried basil

  Dash ground nutmeg

  Salt and pepper to taste

- 2 tablespoons grated Parmesan cheese

In a skillet, saute onion in butter. Add the spinach, soup, eggs, mushrooms, crumbs, feta cheese, oregano, basil, nutmeg, salt and pepper. Spoon into a greased 9-in. square baking pan. Sprinkle with Parmesan cheese.

Bake, uncovered, at 325° for 45-50 minutes or until a knife inserted near the center comes out clean. Cut into 1-in. squares.

YIELD: about 6$\frac{1}{2}$ dozen.

MUSHROOM BURGER CUPS

LUCILLE METCALFE, BARRIE, ONTARIO

PREP: 25 min. BAKE: 35 min.

- 18 slices bread, crusts removed
- $\frac{1}{4}$ cup butter, softened
- 1 pound ground beef, cooked and drained
- 1 can (10 $\frac{3}{4}$ ounces) condensed cream of mushroom soup, undiluted
- 1 egg, beaten
- $\frac{1}{2}$ cup shredded cheddar cheese
- $\frac{1}{4}$ cup chopped onion
- 1 teaspoon Worcestershire sauce

  Salt and pepper to taste

Using a biscuit cutter, cut 2$\frac{1}{2}$-in. circles from bread slices. Spread butter over one side of each circle. Press circles, buttered side down, into ungreased miniature muffin cups.

In a bowl, combine the remaining ingredients. Spoon into bread cups. Bake at 350° for 35 minutes or until golden brown.

YIELD: 1$\frac{1}{2}$ dozen.

CRAB CHEESE FONDUE

MARY HOUCHIN, SWANSEA, ILLINOIS

PREP/TOTAL TIME: 15 min.

3/4	cup milk
1/2	cup condensed cream of mushroom *or* celery soup, undiluted
2	cups (8 ounces) shredded cheddar cheese
8	ounces process cheese (Velveeta), cubed
1	can (6 ounces) crabmeat, drained, flaked and cartilage removed
2	teaspoons lemon juice
1	garlic clove, halved
	Cubed French bread, cherry tomatoes, baby zucchini, cooked new potatoes *and/or* artichoke hearts for dipping

In a saucepan, combine milk and soup until blended. Add cheeses; cook and stir over low heat until melted. Stir in crab and lemon juice; remove from the heat.

Rub the interior of a fondue pot with the cut side of garlic; discard garlic. Pour cheese mixture into pot; keep at a gentle simmer over low heat. Serve with bread cubes, tomatoes, zucchini, potatoes and/or artichoke hearts.

YIELD: 3 cups.

HOT 'N' CHEESY CHICKEN SANDWICHES

NANCY FREDERIKSEN, SPRINGFIELD, MINNESOTA

PREP: 10 min. **BAKE:** 45 min.

6	cups cubed cooked chicken
1 1/2	cups chopped celery
1	can (10 3/4 ounces) condensed cream of mushroom soup, undiluted
3/4	cup mayonnaise
3/4	cup chopped green pepper
1	teaspoon ground mustard
1/2	teaspoon salt
1/2	teaspoon pepper
3	cups cubed process American cheese
24	hamburger buns, split

In a large bowl, combine the first nine ingredients; mix well. Pour into an ungreased 2 1/2-qt. baking dish; top with cheese.

Cover and bake at 350° for 45 minutes or until bubbly. Let stand for 5 minutes; spoon 1/3 cup onto each bun.

YIELD: 24 servings.

EDITOR'S NOTE: Reduced-fat or fat-free mayonnaise is not recommended for this recipe.

SAVORY HERB CHEESECAKE

LEE-ANNE HAMILTON, LOUISBURG, KANSAS

PREP: 15 min. COOK: 35 min. + chilling

- 3 packages (8 ounces *each*) reduced-fat cream cheese, cubed
- 2 cups (16 ounces) reduced-fat sour cream, *divided*
- 1 can (10 ¾ ounces) reduced-fat condensed cream of broccoli soup, undiluted
- ¾ cup egg substitute
- ½ cup grated Romano cheese
- 2 to 4 tablespoons minced fresh basil
- 1 to 2 tablespoons minced fresh thyme
- 1 tablespoon cornstarch
- 1 to 2 teaspoons minced fresh tarragon
- 2 garlic cloves, minced
- ½ teaspoon coarsely ground pepper
- 3 tablespoons *each* chopped sweet red, yellow and orange peppers
- 3 tablespoons minced chives
  Assorted crackers *or* fresh vegetables

In a large mixing bowl, combine the cream cheese, 1 cup sour cream and soup; beat until smooth. Add egg substitute; beat on low just until combined. Add the Romano cheese, basil, thyme, cornstarch, tarragon, garlic and pepper; beat just until blended.

Pour into a 9-in. springform pan coated with nonstick cooking spray. Place pan on a baking sheet. Bake at 350° for 35-45 minutes or until center is almost set. Turn oven off; leave cheesecake in oven with door ajar for 30 minutes.

Remove from oven. Carefully run a knife around edge of pan to loosen. Cool 1 hour longer. Refrigerate overnight. Remove sides of pan. Just before serving, spread with remaining sour cream. Garnish with chopped peppers and chives. Serve with crackers or fresh vegetables.

YIELD: 24 servings.

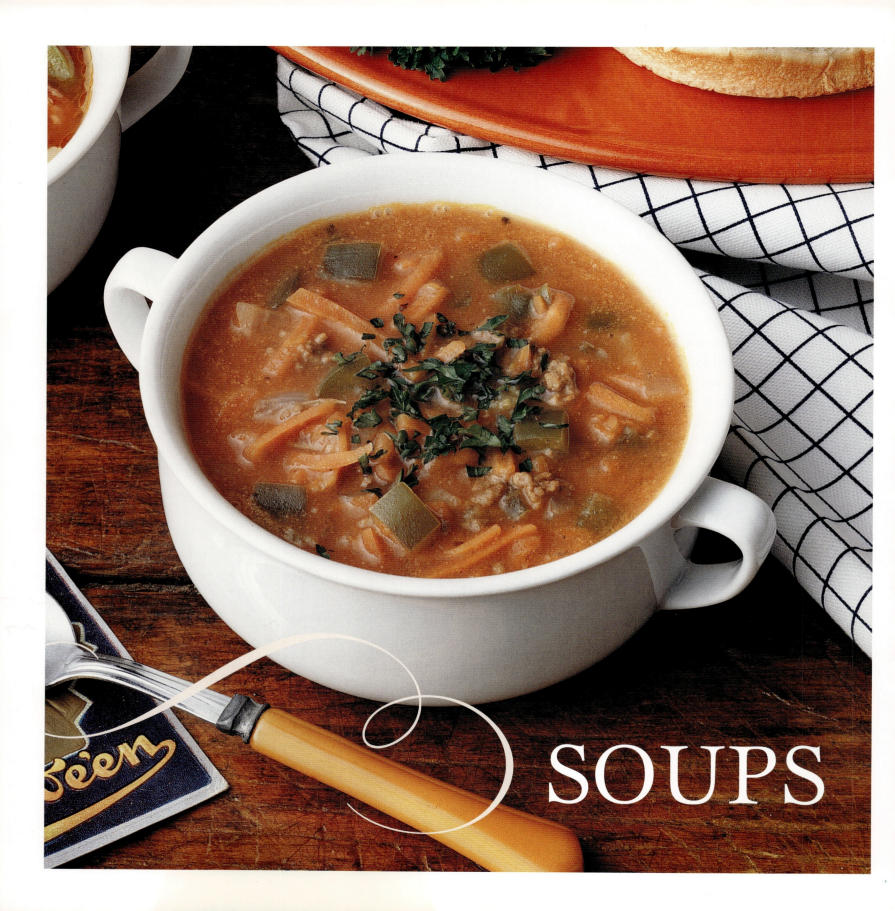

SOUPS

CARROT CHOWDER (pictured left)

WENDY WILKINS, PRATTVILLE, ALABAMA

PREP: 10 min. **COOK:** 1 hour

1	pound ground beef, browned and drained
1/2	cup chopped celery
1/2	cup chopped onion
1	cup chopped green pepper
2 1/2	cups grated carrots
1	can (32 ounces) tomato juice
2	cans (10 3/4 ounces *each*) condensed cream of celery soup, undiluted
1 1/2	cups water
1/2	teaspoon garlic salt
1/2	teaspoon dried marjoram
1	teaspoon sugar
1/2	teaspoon salt
	Shredded Monterey Jack cheese

In a Dutch oven, combine the first 12 ingredients. Bring to a boil. Reduce heat; simmer, uncovered, about 1 hour or until the vegetables are tender. Sprinkle each serving with cheese.

YIELD: 8-10 servings (10 cups).

TOMATO HAMBURGER SOUP

JULIE KRUGER, ST. CLOUD, MINNESOTA

PREP: 5 min. **COOK:** 4 hours

1	can (46 ounces) V8 juice
2	packages (16 ounces *each*) frozen mixed vegetables
1	pound ground beef, cooked and drained
1	can (10 3/4 ounces) condensed cream of mushroom soup, undiluted
2	teaspoons dried minced onion
	Salt and pepper to taste

In a 5-qt. slow cooker, combine the juice, vegetables, beef, soup and onion. Cover and cook on high for 4 hours or until heated through. Season with salt and pepper.

YIELD: 12 servings (3 quarts).

CHICKEN AND DUMPLING SOUP

JOEY ANN MOSTOWY, BRUIN, PENNSYLVANIA

PREP: 15 min. **COOK:** 1 3/4 hours + cooling

6	pieces bone-in chicken
1 1/2	quarts water
2	celery ribs, cut into chunks
1	medium onion, cut into chunks
1/2	cup diced green pepper
1	garlic clove, minced
1	tablespoon minced fresh dill
1	teaspoon salt
1/2	teaspoon pepper
1	can (10 3/4 ounces) condensed cream of potato soup, undiluted
1	can (10 3/4 ounces) condensed cream of chicken soup, undiluted
1	package (10 ounces) frozen mixed vegetables, thawed
1	tube (7 1/2 ounces) refrigerated buttermilk biscuits

In a Dutch oven, combine the first nine ingredients; bring to a boil. Reduce heat; cover and simmer for 40-50 minutes or until chicken is tender. Remove chicken from broth; allow to cool.

Remove chicken from bones; discard bones. Cut chicken into chunks and set aside. Strain broth, discarding vegetables and set aside.

In a large saucepan, combine soups. Gradually add broth, stirring constantly. Add mixed vegetables and reserved chicken; cook over medium heat for 20-30 minutes or until vegetables are tender.

On a floured board, pat biscuits to 1/4-in. thickness; cut into 1/4-in. strips. Bring soup to boil; drop in strips. Cover and cook for 15-18 minutes.

YIELD: 8-10 servings (2 1/2 quarts).

CRAB BISQUE

SHERRIE MANTON, FOLSOM, LOUISIANA

PREP/TOTAL TIME: 15 min.

1	celery rib, thinly sliced
1	small onion, chopped
1/2	cup chopped green pepper
3	tablespoons butter
2	cans (14 3/4 ounces *each*) cream-style corn
2	cans (10 3/4 ounces *each*) condensed cream of potato soup, undiluted
1 1/2	cups milk
1 1/2	cups half-and-half cream
2	bay leaves
1	teaspoon dried thyme
1/2	teaspoon garlic powder
1/4	teaspoon white pepper
1/8	teaspoon hot pepper sauce
3	cans (6 ounces *each*) crabmeat, drained, flaked and cartilage removed

In a large saucepan or Dutch oven, saute celery, onion and green pepper in butter until tender. Add the corn, soup, milk, cream and seasonings; mix well. Stir in crab; heat through. Discard bay leaves. Transfer to a freezer container; cover and freeze for up to 3 months.

TO USE FROZEN SOUP: Thaw in the refrigerator; place in a saucepan and heat through.

YIELD: 10 servings.

Meatball Mushroom Soup

JOANN ABBOTT, KERHONKSON, NEW YORK

PREP/TOTAL TIME: 30 min.

1/2	pound ground beef
2	cans (10 3/4 ounces *each*) condensed cream of mushroom soup, undiluted
1 1/3	cups milk
1 1/3	cups water
1	teaspoon Italian seasoning
1	teaspoon dried minced onion
1/2	teaspoon dried minced garlic
1/4	cup quick-cooking barley
1/4	cup uncooked elbow macaroni
1/4	cup uncooked long grain rice
1	medium carrot, shredded
1	jar (4 1/2 ounces) sliced mushrooms, drained
2	tablespoons grated Parmesan cheese

Shape beef into 1-in. balls; set aside. In a large saucepan, combine the soup, milk and water; bring to a boil. Add the Italian seasoning, onion, garlic, barley, macaroni and rice. Reduce heat; simmer, uncovered, for 15 minutes.

Meanwhile, brown meatballs in a nonstick skillet until no longer pink. Stir carrot into soup; cover and simmer for 5 minutes. Use a slotted spoon to transfer meatballs to soup. Stir in mushrooms and Parmesan cheese; heat through.

YIELD: 6 servings.

SAUSAGE BROCCOLI CHOWDER

DONALD ROBERTS, AMHERST, NEW HAMPSHIRE

PREP/TOTAL TIME: 30 min.

1	pound bulk Italian sausage
1	medium onion, chopped
3	garlic cloves, minced
8	ounces fresh mushrooms, sliced
2	tablespoons butter
2	cups broccoli florets
2	to 3 carrots, diced
2	cans (14 1/2 ounces *each*) chicken broth
1	can (10 3/4 ounces) condensed cream of mushroom soup, undiluted
9	ounces cheese tortellini, cooked and drained
1/2	teaspoon pepper
1/2	teaspoon dried basil
1/2	teaspoon dried thyme
2	quarts half-and-half cream
1/2	cup grated Romano cheese

Crumble sausage into a large skillet; cook over medium heat until no longer pink. Remove to paper towels to drain; set aside.

In the same skillet, saute onion, garlic and mushrooms in butter until tender; set aside. In a Dutch oven or soup kettle, cook the broccoli and carrots in chicken broth until tender. Stir in sausage and the mushroom mixture. Add the soup, tortellini, pepper, basil and thyme; heat through. Stir in cream and Romano cheese; heat through (do not boil).

YIELD: 12-16 servings (4 quarts).

POLISH SAUSAGE SOUP

KRISTIE FRANKLIN, POWELL, WYOMING

PREP/TOTAL TIME: 25 min.

1/2	pound smoked Polish sausage, cubed
1	can (14 1/2 ounces) Cajun-style stewed tomatoes
1	can (11 1/2 ounces) condensed bean with bacon soup, undiluted
1	can (10 3/4 ounces) condensed cream of potato soup, undiluted
2	cups water
1/2	teaspoon dried basil

In a large saucepan, brown sausage over medium heat; drain. Stir in remaining ingredients; bring to a boil. Reduce heat; cover and simmer for 10 minutes.

YIELD: 4-6 servings.

Festive Corn Soup

MRS. OLLIE JAMESON, JEFFERSON, LOUISIANA

PREP: 10 min. **BAKE:** 55 min.

½	cup all-purpose flour
½	cup vegetable oil
1	medium onion, chopped
3	celery ribs, chopped
1	medium green pepper, chopped
½	cup sliced green onions
2	garlic cloves, minced
3	cans (14½ ounces *each*) chicken broth
2	cans (10¾ ounces *each*) condensed cream of corn soup, undiluted
1	can (10 ounces) diced tomatoes with green chilies
1	bay leaf
1	teaspoon salt
¼	to ½ teaspoon white pepper
¼	teaspoon cayenne pepper
	Dash hot pepper sauce
1	pound peeled deveined shrimp
⅓	cup chopped fresh parsley
	Cooked rice

In a Dutch oven, stir flour and oil until smooth. Cook over medium-low heat until mixture is a light reddish-brown, about 10-15 minutes, stirring constantly.

Stir in the onion, celery, green pepper, green onions and garlic. Cook over medium heat until the vegetables are just crisp-tender, about 5 minutes, stirring often. Stir in the broth, soup, tomatoes and seasonings; bring to a boil. Reduce heat; cover and simmer for 30 minutes.

Add shrimp; cook for about 10 minutes longer or until shrimp turn pink, stirring occasionally. Discard bay leaf. Stir in parsley. Serve soup in bowls over rice.

YIELD: 8-10 servings (2½ quarts).

White Chili

GLORIA HUTCHINGS, TROY, MICHIGAN

PREP: 20 min. + standing **COOK:** 1 hour

1	pound dry navy beans
1	medium onion, chopped
2	garlic cloves, minced
1	tablespoon vegetable oil
1	can (10¾ ounces) condensed cream of chicken soup, undiluted
1	can (10¾ ounces) condensed cream of celery soup, undiluted
1	cup water
1	medium potato, peeled and cubed
2	tablespoons chili powder
1	chicken bouillon cube
½	teaspoon salt
1	can (15 ounces) garbanzo beans, rinsed and drained
1½	cups half-and-half cream

Place navy beans in a Dutch oven or soup kettle; add water to cover by 2 in. Bring to a boil; boil for 2 minutes. Remove from the heat; cover and let stand for 1 to 4 hours or until beans are softened. Drain and rinse beans, discarding liquid.

Return beans to pan. Add water to cover by 2 in. Bring to a boil; cover and simmer for 45 minutes or until beans are tender. Drain and discard liquid; set the beans aside.

In the same Dutch oven, saute onion and garlic in oil until tender. Add the soups, 1 cup water, potato, chili powder, bouillon and salt; cover and cook over medium-low heat for 10 minutes. Add the garbanzo beans, cream and navy beans. Cook over medium heat for 10 minutes or until heated through (do not boil).

YIELD: 10 servings.

CHEESY WILD RICE SOUP

LISA HOFER, HITCHCOCK, SOUTH DAKOTA

PREP/TOTAL TIME: 30 min.

1	package (6.2 ounces) fast-cooking long grain and wild rice mix
4	cups milk
1	can (10 ¾ ounces) condensed cream of potato soup, undiluted
8	ounces process cheese (Velveeta), cubed
½	pound sliced bacon, cooked and crumbled

In a large saucepan, prepare rice according to package directions. Stir in the milk, soup and cheese. Cook and stir until cheese is melted. Garnish with bacon.

YIELD: 8 servings.

COOKING TIP

A ½ pound of cubed Brie, in place of the process cheese, would add a rich, buttery flavor to this soup.

COUNTRY POTATO CHOWDER

SARA PHILLIPS, TOPEKA, KANSAS

PREP: 30 min. **COOK:** 40 min.

- 6 bacon strips, diced
- 1 medium onion, chopped
- 3 celery ribs, chopped
- 1/4 cup all-purpose flour
- 1 quart half-and-half cream
- 4 medium potatoes, peeled and cut into 1/2-inch cubes
- 2 cans (10 3/4 ounces *each*) condensed cream of celery soup, undiluted
- 2 tablespoons dried parsley flakes
- 1 tablespoon Worcestershire sauce
- 1 teaspoon seasoned salt
- 1/2 teaspoon pepper
- 1 cup sliced carrots
- 1 cup fresh *or* frozen green beans, cut into 2-inch pieces
- 1 can (14 3/4 ounces) cream-style corn

In a Dutch oven, cook bacon over medium heat until crisp. Using a slotted spoon, remove to paper towels. Drain, reserving 2 tablespoons drippings.

In the drippings, saute onion and celery until tender. Sprinkle with flour and stir until blended. Gradually add cream. Stir in the potatoes, soup, parsley, Worcestershire sauce, seasoned salt and pepper. Bring to a boil; cook and stir for 1 minute. Reduce heat; cover and simmer for 25 minutes, stirring occasionally.

Add the carrots and beans. Cover and simmer 15 minutes longer or until the vegetables are tender. Stir in corn and reserved bacon; heat through.

YIELD: 12 servings.

CHEESY ASPARAGUS SOUP

PATRICIA LOCKARD, ROCKFORD, MICHIGAN

PREP/TOTAL TIME: 25 min.

- 3 pounds fresh asparagus, trimmed
- 1 small onion, chopped
- 2 cans (10 3/4 ounces *each*) condensed cream of asparagus soup, undiluted
- 2 soup cans milk
- 1 jar (4 1/2 ounces) sliced mushrooms, drained
- 3 cups (12 ounces) shredded cheddar cheese

Place 2 in. of water in a large kettle; add asparagus and onion. Bring to a boil. Reduce heat; cover and simmer 3-5 minutes or until tender. Drain liquid.

Add the remaining ingredients; heat over medium until the cheese is melted and the soup is hot.

YIELD: 8-10 servings.

CORNY CLAM CHOWDER

KAREN JOHNSTON, SYRACUSE, NEBRASKA

PREP/TOTAL TIME: 15 min.

- 1 can (14 3/4 ounces) cream-style corn
- 1 can (10 3/4 ounces) condensed cream of potato soup, undiluted
- 1 1/2 cups half-and-half cream
- 1 can (6 1/2 ounces) minced clams, drained
- 6 bacon strips, cooked and crumbled

In a saucepan, combine the corn, soup and cream; heat through. Stir in clams; heat through. Garnish with bacon.

YIELD: 4 servings.

CREAM OF HAMBURGER SOUP

CLAUDETTE RENARD, GREEN BAY, WISCONSIN

PREP: 15 min. **COOK:** 65 min.

- 1½ cups water
- 1 cup sliced carrots
- 1 cup sliced celery
- 1 cup cubed peeled potatoes
- ¼ cup chopped onion
- 1 pound ground beef, cooked and drained
- 1 can (10 ¾ ounces) condensed cream of mushroom soup, undiluted
- 1 can (10 ¾ ounces) condensed cream of potato soup, undiluted
- 1 tablespoon chili powder
- 1 teaspoon dried parsley flakes
- ¼ teaspoon *each* paprika, garlic salt, seasoned salt and pepper
- 3 cups milk

In a large saucepan or Dutch oven, combine water, carrots, celery, potatoes and onion; bring to a boil over medium heat. Reduce heat; cover and simmer for 15-20 minutes or until vegetables are tender.

Add the beef, soups and seasonings; bring to a boil. Reduce heat; cover and simmer for 45 minutes, stirring occasionally. Stir in milk; heat through (do not boil).

YIELD: 10 servings (2¼ quarts).

REUBEN CHOWDER

IOLA EGLE, BELLA VISTA, ARKANSAS

PREP/TOTAL TIME: 30 min.

- 1 tablespoon butter, softened
- 3 slices rye bread
- 1 can (11 ounces) condensed nacho cheese soup, undiluted
- 1 can (10 ¾ ounces) condensed cream of mushroom soup, undiluted
- 3 cups milk
- 1 can (14 ounces) sauerkraut, rinsed and drained
- 12 ounces deli corned beef, diced
- 1 cup (4 ounces) shredded part-skim mozzarella cheese

Butter bread on both sides, then cut into cubes. Place on an ungreased baking sheet. Bake at 375° for 6-8 minutes or until browned.

Meanwhile, in a large saucepan, combine the soups, milk, sauerkraut and corned beef; cook and stir over medium heat for 8-10 minutes or until heated through. Add cheese; stir until melted. Top with croutons.

YIELD: 8 servings (2 quarts).

SOOTHING CHICKEN SOUP

KRIS COUNTRYMAN, JOLIET, ILLINOIS

PREP/TOTAL TIME: 20 min.

- 2 cups sliced celery
- 3 quarts chicken broth
- 4 cups cubed cooked chicken
- 1 can (10 ¾ ounces) condensed cream of mushroom soup, undiluted
- 1 cup uncooked instant rice
- 1 envelope onion soup mix
- 1 teaspoon poultry seasoning
- ½ teaspoon seasoned salt
- ½ teaspoon dried thyme
- ½ teaspoon pepper

In a Dutch oven or soup kettle, bring celery and broth to a boil. Reduce heat; simmer, uncovered, until tender.

Stir in the remaining ingredients. Bring to a boil. Reduce heat; cover and simmer for 6-8 minutes or until the rice is tender.

YIELD: 16 servings (4 quarts).

Broccoli Wild Rice Soup

JANET SAWYER, DYSART, IOWA

PREP/TOTAL TIME: 30 min.

- 1 package (6 ounces) chicken and wild rice mix
- 5 cups water
- 1 package (10 ounces) frozen chopped broccoli, thawed
- 1 medium carrot, shredded
- 2 teaspoons dried minced onion
- 1 can (10 3/4 ounces) condensed cream of chicken soup, undiluted
- 1 package (8 ounces) cream cheese, cubed
- 1/4 cup slivered almonds, optional

In a large saucepan, combine the rice, contents of seasoning packet and water; bring to a boil. Reduce heat; cover and simmer for 10 minutes, stirring once.

Stir in the broccoli, carrot and onion. Cover and simmer for 5 minutes. Stir in soup and cream cheese. Cook and stir until cheese is melted. Stir in almonds if desired.

YIELD: 8 servings (about 2 quarts).

Pantry-Shelf Salmon Chowder

KATHRYN AWE, INTERNATIONAL FALLS, MINNESOTA

PREP/TOTAL TIME: 20 min.

- 1 small onion, thinly sliced
- 1 tablespoon butter
- 1 can (10 3/4 ounces) condensed cream of celery soup, undiluted
- 1 1/3 cups milk
- 1 can (7 1/2 ounces) salmon, drained, bones and skin removed
- 1 can (15 ounces) cream-style corn
- 1 tablespoon minced fresh parsley

In a large saucepan, saute onion in butter until tender. Stir in remaining ingredients; heat through.

YIELD: 4 servings.

BEEF AND BACON CHOWDER

NANCY SCHMIDT, CENTER, COLORADO

PREP/TOTAL TIME: 30 min.

1	pound ground beef
2	cups chopped celery
1/2	cup chopped onion
4	cups milk
3	cups cubed peeled potatoes, cooked
2	cans (10 3/4 ounces *each*) condensed cream of mushroom soup, undiluted
2	cups chopped carrots, cooked
	Salt and pepper to taste
12	bacon strips, cooked and crumbled

In a Dutch oven, cook the beef, celery and onion over medium heat until the meat is no longer pink and the vegetables are tender; drain.

Add the milk, potatoes, soup, carrots, salt and pepper; heat through. Stir in the bacon just before serving.

YIELD: 12 servings (3 quarts).

BROCCOLI CHEESE SOUP

GLADYS SCHULER, BISMARCK, NORTH DAKOTA

PREP/TOTAL TIME: 25 min.

1/2	cup shredded carrot
2	tablespoons finely chopped onion
2	tablespoons butter
2	cups milk
1	cup water
1	package (10 ounces) frozen chopped broccoli
1/8	teaspoon pepper
2	cans (10 3/4 ounces *each*) condensed cream of potato soup, undiluted
1	cup (4 ounces) shredded cheddar cheese

In a large saucepan, saute carrot and onion in butter until carrot is tender. Add the milk, water, broccoli and pepper; simmer, uncovered, for 10 minutes or until broccoli is tender, stirring occasionally.

Add soup and cheese; cook over low heat until soup is heated through and cheese is melted.

YIELD: 6 servings.

SEAFOOD BISQUE

PAT EDWARDS, DAUPHIN ISLAND, ALABAMA

PREP/TOTAL TIME: 30 min.

2	cans (10 3/4 ounces *each*) condensed cream of mushroom soup, undiluted
1	can (10 3/4 ounces) condensed cream of celery soup, undiluted
2 2/3	cups milk
4	green onions, chopped
1/2	cup finely chopped celery
1	garlic clove, minced
1	teaspoon Worcestershire sauce
1/4	teaspoon hot pepper sauce
1 1/2	pounds uncooked medium shrimp, peeled and deveined
1	can (6 ounces) crabmeat, drained, flaked and cartilage removed
1	jar (4 1/2 ounces) whole mushrooms, drained
3	tablespoons Madeira wine *or* chicken broth
1/2	teaspoon salt
1/2	teaspoon pepper
	Minced fresh parsley

In a Dutch oven, combine the first eight ingredients. Bring to a boil. Reduce heat; add the shrimp, crab and mushrooms. Simmer, uncovered, for 10 minutes.

Stir in the wine or broth, salt and pepper; cook 2-3 minutes longer. Garnish with parsley.

YIELD: 10 servings (2 1/2 quarts).

LEMON CHICKEN SOUP

JOAN FOTOPOULOS, TURAH, MONTANA

PREP/TOTAL TIME: 10 min.

1	can (10 1/2 ounces) condensed chicken with rice soup, undiluted
1	can (10 3/4 ounces) condensed cream of chicken soup, undiluted
2 1/4	cups water
1	cup diced cooked chicken, optional
1	to 2 tablespoons lemon juice
	Pepper to taste
	Minced fresh parsley, optional

In a large saucepan, combine soups and water. Heat through. Add the chicken if desired. Stir in lemon juice and pepper. Garnish with parsley if desired.

YIELD: 4-5 servings.

Enchilada Chicken Soup

CRISTIN FISCHER, BELLEVUE, NEBRASKA

PREP/TOTAL TIME: 10 min.

- 1 can (11 ounces) condensed nacho cheese soup, undiluted
- 1 can (10 3/4 ounces) condensed cream of chicken soup, undiluted
- 2 2/3 cups milk
- 1 can (10 ounces) chunk white chicken, drained
- 1 can (10 ounces) enchilada sauce
- 1 can (4 ounces) chopped green chilies
  Sour cream

In a large saucepan, combine the soups, milk, chicken, enchilada sauce and chilies. Cook until heated through. Garnish with sour cream.

YIELD: 7 servings.

Rosemary Mushroom Soup

SANDRA BURROWS, COVENTRY, CONNECTICUT

PREP/TOTAL TIME: 15 min.

- 1 cup sliced fresh mushrooms
- 2 garlic cloves, minced
- 1/4 cup butter
- 1 can (10 3/4 ounces) condensed cream of mushroom soup, undiluted
- 1 cup half-and-half cream
- 1 tablespoon minced fresh rosemary *or* 1 teaspoon dried rosemary, crushed
- 1/2 teaspoon paprika
- 2 tablespoons minced chives

In a large saucepan, saute mushrooms and garlic in butter until tender. Stir in mushroom soup, cream, rosemary and paprika; heat through but do not boil. Sprinkle with chives.

YIELD: 3 servings.

Broccoli-Cauliflower Cheese Soup

JANET HALL, PLEASANT VALLEY, IOWA

PREP: 15 min. **COOK:** 50 min.

- 3 quarts water
- 8 chicken bouillon cubes
- 2 1/2 cups diced peeled potatoes
- 1 cup chopped celery
- 1/2 cup chopped onion
- 2 packages (10 ounces *each*) frozen chopped broccoli
- 1 package (16 ounces) frozen cauliflowerets
- 2 cans (10 3/4 ounces *each*) condensed cream of chicken soup, undiluted
- 1 pound process cheese (Velveeta), cubed
- 1/2 teaspoon dried thyme
- 1/4 teaspoon pepper

In a soup kettle or Dutch oven, combine the water, bouillon, potatoes, celery and onion. Bring to a boil. Reduce heat to medium; cook, uncovered, for 20 minutes or until vegetables are almost tender.

Add broccoli and cauliflower; cook over medium heat for 10 minutes. Stir in the soup, cheese, thyme and pepper; simmer for 20 minutes, stirring occasionally.

YIELD: 18-20 servings (about 5 1/2 quarts).

HALIBUT CHOWDER

MARY DAVIS, PALMER, ALASKA

PREP/TOTAL TIME: 20 min.

8	to 10 green onions, thinly sliced
2	garlic cloves, minced
2	tablespoons butter
4	cans (10 ¾ ounces *each*) condensed cream of potato soup, undiluted
2	cans (10 ¾ ounces *each*) condensed cream of mushroom soup, undiluted
4	cups milk
2	packages (8 ounces *each*) cream cheese, cubed
1 ½	pounds halibut *or* salmon fillets, cubed
1 ½	cups frozen sliced carrots
1 ½	cups frozen corn
⅛	to ¼ teaspoon cayenne pepper, optional

In a Dutch oven or soup kettle, saute onions and garlic in butter until tender. Add the soups, milk and cream cheese; cook and stir until cheese is melted.

Stir in the fish, carrots and corn. Bring to a boil. Reduce heat; simmer, uncovered, for 5-10 minutes or until fish flakes easily and the vegetables are tender. Add cayenne pepper if desired.

YIELD: 16 servings (about 4 quarts).

CORN CHOWDER

MURIEL LERDAL, HUMBOLDT, IOWA

PREP: 15 min. **COOK:** 20 min.

¾	cup chopped onion
2	tablespoons butter
1	cup diced cooked peeled potatoes
1	cup diced fully cooked ham
2	cups frozen corn
1	cup cream-style corn
1	can (10 ¾ ounces) condensed cream of mushroom soup, undiluted
2 ½	cups milk
	Salt and pepper to taste
1	tablespoon chopped fresh parsley

In a heavy saucepan, cook the onion in butter until tender. Add all remaining ingredients; bring to a boil. Reduce heat; simmer, uncovered, for 20-30 minutes.

YIELD: 6-8 servings.

COOKING TIP

This chowder recipe would be equally as tasty using cream of potato soup or celery soup for the mushroom soup.

CHILLED POTATO SOUP

SANDRA PICHON, SLIDELL, LOUISIANA

PREP/TOTAL TIME: 10 min.

1 1/3	cups milk
1	can (10 3/4 ounces) condensed cream of potato soup, undiluted
3/4	teaspoon minced fresh basil *or* 1/4 teaspoon dried basil
1/4	teaspoon minced chives
1	cup (8 ounces) sour cream
1/4	cup white wine *or* chicken broth

Place all the ingredients in a blender or food processor; cover and process until smooth. Transfer to a bowl; cover and chill until serving.

YIELD: 4 servings.

ZESTY CHEESEBURGER SOUP

NORMA ROWE, WINFIELD, KANSAS

PREP: 10 min. **COOK:** 35 min.

2	pounds ground beef
1	medium onion, chopped
	Salt, pepper and garlic powder to taste
1 1/2	cups cubed peeled potatoes
1 1/2	cups water
1	can (15 1/4 ounces) whole kernel corn, drained
1	can (14 3/4 ounces) cream-style corn
1	can (11 ounces) condensed cheddar cheese soup, undiluted
1	can (10 3/4 ounces) condensed cream of asparagus soup, undiluted
1	can (10 3/4 ounces) condensed cream of mushroom soup, undiluted
1	can (10 ounces) diced tomatoes and green chilies
2	cups half-and-half cream

In a Dutch oven or soup kettle, cook the beef, onion, salt, pepper and garlic powder over medium heat until meat is no longer pink; drain. Add potatoes and water; bring to a boil. Reduce heat; cover and simmer for 15-20 minutes or until the potatoes are tender.

Add the corn, soups and tomatoes; mix well. Bring to a boil. Reduce heat. Stir in cream; heat through (do not boil).

YIELD: 14-16 servings (3 3/4 quarts).

CHICKEN WILD RICE SOUP

GAYLE HOLDMAN, HIGHLAND, UTAH

PREP/TOTAL TIME: 30 min.

5 2/3	cups water
1	package (4.3 ounces) long grain and wild rice mix
1	envelope chicken noodle soup mix
1	celery rib, chopped
1	medium carrot, chopped
1/3	cup chopped onion
2	cans (10 3/4 ounces *each*) condensed cream of chicken soup, undiluted
1	cup cubed cooked chicken

In a large saucepan, combine the water, rice with contents of seasoning packet and soup mix. Bring to a boil. Reduce heat; cover and simmer for 10 minutes.

Stir in the celery, carrot and onion. Cover and simmer for 10 minutes. Stir in chicken soup and chicken. Cook 8 minutes longer or until the rice and vegetables are tender.

YIELD: 5 servings.

Easy Baked Potato Soup

JULIE SMITHOUSER, COLORADO SPRINGS, COLORADO

PREP/TOTAL TIME: 30 min.

- 3 to 4 medium baking potatoes, baked
- 5 bacon strips, diced
- 2 cans (10 3/4 ounces *each*) condensed cream of potato soup, undiluted
- 1 can (10 3/4 ounces) condensed cheddar cheese soup, undiluted
- 3 1/2 cups milk
- 2 teaspoons garlic powder
- 2 teaspoons Worcestershire sauce
- 1/2 teaspoon onion powder
- 1/4 teaspoon pepper
  Dash Liquid Smoke, optional
- 1 cup (8 ounces) sour cream
  Shredded cheddar cheese

Peel and dice the baked potatoes; set aside. In a Dutch oven, cook the bacon over medium heat until crisp. Using a slotted spoon, remove to paper towels. Drain, reserving 1 1/2 teaspoons drippings.

Add the soups, milk, garlic powder, Worcestershire sauce, onion powder, pepper, Liquid Smoke if desired and reserved potatoes to the drippings. Cook, uncovered, for 10 minutes or until heated through, stirring occasionally.

Stir in sour cream; cook for 1-2 minutes or until heated through (do not boil). Garnish with cheddar cheese and bacon.

YIELD: 10 servings (2 1/2 quarts).

In-a-Hurry Curry Soup

DENISE ELDER, HANOVER, ONTARIO

PREP/TOTAL TIME: 10 min.

- 1 cup chopped onion
- 3/4 teaspoon curry powder
- 2 tablespoons butter
- 2 chicken bouillon cubes
- 1 cup hot water
- 1 can (14 1/2 ounces) diced tomatoes, undrained
- 1 can (10 3/4 ounces) condensed cream of celery soup, undiluted
- 1 cup half-and-half cream
- 1 can (5 ounces) white chicken, drained

In a large saucepan, saute onion and curry powder in butter until onion is tender. Dissolve bouillon in water; add to the saucepan. Stir in remaining ingredients; heat through.

YIELD: about 5 servings.

Quick Clam Chowder

JUDY JUNGWIRTH, ATHOL, SOUTH DAKOTA

PREP/TOTAL TIME: 10 min.

- 1 can (10 3/4 ounces) condensed cream of celery soup, undiluted
- 1 can (10 3/4 ounces) condensed cream of potato soup, undiluted
- 2 cups half-and-half cream
- 2 cans (6 1/2 ounces *each*) minced/chopped clams, drained
- 1/2 teaspoon ground nutmeg
  Pepper to taste

In a large saucepan, combine all ingredients. Cook and stir over medium heat until heated through.

YIELD: 5 servings.

CHICKEN TORTILLA CHOWDER

JENNIFER GOUGE, LUBBOCK, TEXAS

PREP/TOTAL TIME: 20 min.

1	can (14 1/2 ounces) chicken broth
1	can (10 3/4 ounces) condensed cream of chicken soup, undiluted
1	can (10 3/4 ounces) condensed cream of potato soup, undiluted
1 1/2	cups milk
2	cups cubed cooked chicken
1	can (11 ounces) Mexicorn
1	jar (4 1/2 ounces) sliced mushrooms, drained
1	can (4 ounces) chopped green chilies
1/4	cup thinly sliced green onions
4	flour tortillas (6 to 7 inches), cut into 1/2-inch strips
1 1/2	cups (6 ounces) shredded cheddar cheese

In a Dutch oven, combine the broth, soups and milk. Add the chicken, corn, mushrooms, chilies and onions; mix well. Bring to a boil. Add the tortilla strips. Reduce heat; simmer, uncovered, for 8-10 minutes or until heated through. Add cheese; stir just until melted. Serve immediately.

YIELD: 8-10 servings (2 1/2 quarts).

GRANDMA'S CHICKEN 'N' DUMPLING SOUP

PAULETTE BALDA, PROPHETSTOWN, ILLINOIS

PREP: 20 min. **COOK:** 2 hours 50 min.

1	broiler-fryer chicken (3 1/2 to 4 pounds), cut up
2 1/4	quarts cold water
5	chicken bouillon cubes
6	whole peppercorns
3	whole cloves
1	can (10 3/4 ounces) condensed cream of chicken soup, undiluted
1	can (10 3/4 ounces) condensed cream of mushroom soup, undiluted
1 1/2	cups chopped carrots
1	cup fresh *or* frozen peas
1	cup chopped celery
1	cup chopped peeled potatoes
1/4	cup chopped onion
1 1/2	teaspoons seasoned salt
1/4	teaspoon pepper
1	bay leaf

DUMPLINGS:

2	cups all-purpose flour
4	teaspoons baking powder
1	teaspoon salt
1/4	teaspoon pepper
1	egg, beaten
2	tablespoons butter, melted
3/4	to 1 cup milk
	Minced fresh parsley, optional

In an 8-qt. Dutch oven or soup kettle, combine the chicken, water, bouillon, peppercorns and cloves. Cover and slowly bring to a boil; skim fat. Reduce heat; cover and simmer 1 1/2 hours or until chicken is tender.

Remove chicken from broth; allow to cool. Strain broth; return to kettle. Remove chicken from bones; discard bones. Cut chicken into chunks and set aside. Skim fat from broth.

Return chicken to kettle along with the soups, vegetables and seasonings; bring to a boil. Reduce heat; cover and simmer for 1 hour. Uncover; increase heat to a gentle boil. Discard bay leaf.

For dumplings, combine dry ingredients in a medium bowl. Stir in egg, butter and enough milk to make a moist stiff batter. Drop by teaspoonfuls into soup. Cover and simmer for 18-20 minutes or until a toothpick inserted in a dumpling comes out clean (do not lift the cover while simmering). Sprinkle with parsley if desired.

YIELD: 12 servings (3 quarts).

Super-Duper Chili

ELIZABETH MAYS, NUNNELLY, TENNESSEE

PREP: 20 min. COOK: 30 min.

- 1 pound bulk pork sausage
- 1 pound ground beef
- 2 cans (15 1/2 ounces *each*) hot chili beans
- 1 jar (16 ounces) salsa
- 1 can (16 ounces) kidney beans, rinsed and drained
- 1 can (15 ounces) pinto beans, rinsed and drained
- 1 can (14 1/2 ounces) diced tomatoes, undrained
- 1 can (10 3/4 ounces) condensed cream of mushroom soup, undiluted
- 1 can (8 ounces) tomato sauce
- 8 ounces process cheese (Velveeta), cubed
- 1 1/2 teaspoons chili powder
- 1/2 teaspoon cayenne pepper

In a Dutch oven or soup kettle, cook the sausage and beef over medium heat until no longer pink; drain. Stir in the remaining ingredients. Bring to a boil. Reduce heat; cover and simmer for 30 minutes or until heated through.

YIELD: 14 servings (3 1/2 quarts).

Beefy Wild Rice Soup

MARILYN CHESBROUGH, WAUTOMA, WISCONSIN

PREP: 15 min. COOK: 1 1/4 hours

- 1 pound ground beef
- 1/2 teaspoon Italian seasoning
- 6 cups water, *divided*
- 2 large onions, chopped
- 3 celery ribs, chopped
- 1 cup uncooked wild rice
- 2 teaspoons beef bouillon granules

- 1/2 teaspoon pepper
- 1/4 teaspoon hot pepper sauce
- 3 cans (10 3/4 ounces *each*) condensed cream of mushroom soup, undiluted
- 1 can (4 ounces) mushroom stems and pieces, drained

In a Dutch oven, cook beef and Italian seasoning over medium heat until meat is no longer pink; drain. Add 2 cups water, onions, celery, rice, bouillon, pepper and hot pepper sauce; bring to a boil. Reduce heat; cover and simmer for 45 minutes.

Stir in the soup, mushrooms and remaining water. Cover and simmer for 30 minutes.

YIELD: 10-12 servings (3 quarts).

Salmon Chowder

TOM BAILEY, GOLDEN VALLEY, MINNESOTA

PREP/TOTAL TIME: 10 min.

- 3 cans (10 3/4 ounces *each*) condensed cream of potato soup, undiluted
- 2 2/3 cups half-and-half cream
- 1 can (14 3/4 ounces) salmon, drained, bones and skin removed
- 1 teaspoon dill weed
- 1/2 teaspoon salt
- 1/4 teaspoon white pepper
- 1/4 teaspoon crushed red pepper flakes

In a large saucepan, combine all of the ingredients. Cook and stir over medium heat until chowder is heated through.

YIELD: 7 servings.

Hearty Hash Brown Soup

FRANCES RECTOR, VINTON, IOWA

PREP: 10 min. **COOK:** 30 min.

2	pounds frozen shredded hash brown potatoes
4	cups water
1	large onion, chopped
3/4	cup sliced celery
4	chicken bouillon cubes
1/2	teaspoon celery seed
1/4	teaspoon pepper
4	cans (10 3/4 ounces *each*) condensed cream of chicken soup, undiluted
1	quart milk
2	cups cubed fully cooked ham
1	tablespoon dried parsley flakes
1 1/2	teaspoons garlic salt
8	bacon strips, cooked and crumbled

In a Dutch oven or soup kettle, combine the first seven ingredients; bring to a boil. Reduce heat; cover and simmer for 20 minutes or until vegetables are tender.

Mash vegetables with cooking liquid. Add soup and milk; stir until smooth. Add the ham, parsley and garlic salt; simmer for 10 minutes or until heated through. Garnish with the bacon.

YIELD: 12-16 servings (4 quarts).

CHEESY POTATO SOUP

TAMMY CONDIT, LEAGUE CITY, TEXAS

PREP: 10 min. **COOK:** 35 min.

- 1 medium onion, chopped
- 2 tablespoons butter
- 6 medium potatoes, peeled and cubed
- 5 cups water
- 2 cups milk
- 1 can (10 ¾ ounces) condensed cream of chicken soup, undiluted
- ½ teaspoon garlic salt
- ⅛ teaspoon pepper
- 12 ounces process cheese (Velveeta), cubed
  Minced fresh parsley

In a Dutch oven, saute onion in butter. Add potatoes and water. Bring to a boil. Reduce heat; cover and simmer for 15 minutes or until potatoes are tender.

Stir in milk, soup, garlic salt and pepper; heat through. Add cheese; stir until cheese is melted. Garnish with parsley.

YIELD: 10 servings (2½ quarts).

CHICKEN AND BACON CHOWDER

NANCY SCHMIDT, DELHI, CALIFORNIA

PREP: 15 min. **COOK:** 40 min.

- 1 pound sliced bacon
- 3 cups diced celery
- ½ cup diced onion
- 4 cups diced peeled potatoes
- 3 cups chicken broth
- 2 cups diced carrots
- 3 cups diced cooked chicken
- 2 cans (10 ¾ ounces *each*) condensed cream of mushroom soup, undiluted

- 2 cups half-and-half cream
- ½ teaspoon salt
- ½ teaspoon pepper

In a Dutch oven, cook bacon over medium heat until crisp. Drain, reserving 2 tablespoons drippings. Crumble bacon and set aside.

Saute celery and onion in reserved drippings until tender. Add the potatoes, broth and carrots; bring to a boil. Reduce heat; cover and simmer for 20 minutes or until vegetables are tender. Stir in remaining ingredients and heat through.

YIELD: 12 servings (3 quarts).

SAUSAGE CORN CHOWDER

SHARON WALLACE, OMAHA, NEBRASKA

PREP/TOTAL TIME: 25 min.

- 2 packages (7 ounces *each*) pork *or* turkey breakfast sausage
- 2 cans (10 ¾ ounces *each*) condensed cream of chicken soup, undiluted
- 2 ½ cups milk
- 2 cups fresh corn
- ⅔ cup sliced green onions
- ½ teaspoon hot pepper sauce
- 1 cup (4 ounces) shredded Swiss cheese

Crumble sausage into a large saucepan or Dutch oven; cook over medium heat until no longer pink. Drain. Add the soup, milk, corn, onions and hot pepper sauce. Cook until corn is tender. Reduce heat to low; add cheese and stir until cheese is melted.

YIELD: 6-8 servings (2 quarts).

BRUNCH

SAUSAGE HASH BROWN BAKE (pictured left)

ESTHER WRINKLES, VANZANT, MISSOURI

PREP: 15 min. **BAKE:** 55 min.

- 2 pounds bulk pork sausage
- 2 cups (8 ounces) shredded cheddar cheese, *divided*
- 1 can (10 3/4 ounces) condensed cream of chicken soup, undiluted
- 1 cup (8 ounces) sour cream
- 1 carton (8 ounces) French onion dip
- 1 cup chopped onion
- 1/4 cup chopped green pepper
- 1/4 cup chopped sweet red pepper
- 1/8 teaspoon pepper
- 1 package (30 ounces) frozen shredded hash brown potatoes, thawed

In a large skillet, cook sausage over medium heat until no longer pink; drain on paper towels. In a large bowl, combine 1 3/4 cups cheese and the next seven ingredients; fold in potatoes.

Spread half into a greased shallow 3-qt. baking dish. Top with sausage and remaining potato mixture. Sprinkle with remaining cheese. Cover and bake at 350° for 45 minutes. Uncover; bake 10 minutes longer or until heated through.

YIELD: 10-12 servings.

HAM MUSHROOM PIE

HOWIE WIENER, SPRING HILL, FLORIDA

PREP: 15 min. **BAKE:** 35 min.

- 1 boneless fully cooked ham steak (about 1 pound)
- 1 pastry shell (9 inches), baked
- 2/3 cup condensed cream of mushroom soup, undiluted
- 2/3 cup sour cream
- 3 eggs, lightly beaten
- 2 tablespoons minced chives
  Dash pepper

Cut ham to fit the bottom of pastry shell; place in shell. In a bowl, combine the remaining ingredients. Pour over ham. Cover edges loosely with foil.

Bake at 425° for 35-40 minutes or until a knife inserted near the center comes out clean. Let stand for 5 minutes before cutting.

YIELD: 6 servings.

Remove and discard crust from bread if desired. Butter bread; cube and place in a greased 13-in. x 9-in. x 2-in. baking dish. Sprinkle with the cheese, sausage, red pepper and onions in order given. In a bowl, beat eggs. Add the soup, milk, wine or additional milk, mustard and pepper. Pour over bread mixture; cover and refrigerate overnight.

Remove from the refrigerator 30 minutes before baking. Bake, uncovered, at 325° for 45-60 minutes or until a knife comes out clean. Let stand for 5 minutes before cutting.

YIELD: **8-10 servings.**

SUNDAY BRUNCH CASSEROLE

ROY LYON, COUPEVILLE, WASHINGTON

PREP: 15 min. **BAKE:** 45 min.

6	slices sourdough *or* day-old white bread
3	to 4 tablespoons butter, softened
2	cups (8 ounces) shredded cheddar cheese
1	pound bulk pork sausage, cooked and drained
1/2	medium sweet red pepper, cut into thin strips
1/4	cup sliced green onion tops
3	eggs
1	can (10 3/4 ounces) condensed cream of asparagus soup, undiluted
2	cups milk
1/4	cup dry white wine *or* additional milk
1/2	teaspoon Dijon mustard
1/4	teaspoon pepper

FAST AND FLAVORFUL EGGS

MICHELE CHRISTMAN, SIDNEY, ILLINOIS

PREP/TOTAL TIME: 25 min.

1/4	cup chopped green pepper
1	tablespoon butter
6	eggs, lightly beaten
1	can (10 3/4 ounces) condensed cream of chicken soup, undiluted, *divided*
3/4	teaspoon salt
1/2	teaspoon pepper
6	bacon strips, cooked and crumbled
1/2	cup milk

In a skillet, saute green pepper in butter until tender. Combine the eggs, 1/2 cup soup, salt and pepper. Add to skillet; cook and stir gently until the eggs are set. Stir in bacon.

For sauce, heat milk and remaining soup; stir until smooth. Serve over eggs.

YIELD: **3-4 servings.**

COOKING TIP | Fresh eggs should be stored in their carton in the refrigerator. The carton acts as a cushion and helps prevent breakage.

BAKED STUFFED EGGS

LORRAINE BYLSMA, EUTIS, FLORIDA

PREP: 15 min. + chilling **BAKE:** 25 min.

STUFFED EGGS:

8	hard-cooked eggs
3	to 4 tablespoons sour cream
2	teaspoons prepared mustard
$\frac{1}{2}$	teaspoon salt

SAUCE:

$\frac{1}{2}$	cup chopped onion
2	tablespoons butter
1	can (10 $\frac{3}{4}$ ounces) condensed cream of mushroom soup, undiluted
1	cup (8 ounces) sour cream
$\frac{1}{2}$	cup shredded cheddar cheese
$\frac{1}{2}$	teaspoon paprika

Slice eggs in half lengthwise; remove yolks and set whites aside. In a bowl, mash yolks with a fork. Add the sour cream, mustard and salt; mix well. Fill the egg whites; set aside.

In a saucepan, saute onion in butter until tender. Add soup and sour cream; mix well. Pour half into an ungreased 11-in. x 7-in. x 2-in. baking dish. Arrange stuffed eggs over the sauce. Spoon remaining sauce on top. Sprinkle with cheese and paprika. Cover and refrigerate overnight.

Remove from the refrigerator 30 minutes before baking. Bake, uncovered, at 350° for 25-30 minutes or until heated through. Serve immediately.

YIELD: 6-8 servings.

EGGS DELMONICO

EDIE FARM, FARMINGTON, NEW MEXICO

PREP/TOTAL TIME: 10 min.

- 1   can (10 ¾ ounces) condensed cream of mushroom *or* cream of chicken soup, undiluted
- ½   cup shredded cheddar cheese
- 3   hard-cooked eggs, sliced
- 1   tablespoon finely chopped pimientos
- 4   pieces toast *or* 2 English muffins, split and toasted

  Paprika *or* minced fresh parsley

In a saucepan, heat soup over medium heat until hot and bubbly. Reduce heat; stir in cheese. Cook and stir until cheese is melted. Fold in eggs and pimientos; cook until heated through. Serve over toast or English muffins. Garnish with paprika or parsley.

YIELD: 2 servings.

HOBO HASH

LINDA HENDERSHOTT, ST. JOSEPH, MICHIGAN

PREP/TOTAL TIME: 30 min.

- ½   pound sliced bacon, diced
- 1   medium onion, chopped
- 1   cup sliced fresh mushrooms
- 5   medium potatoes, peeled, cubed and cooked
- 1   can (10 ¾ ounces) condensed cream of mushroom soup, undiluted

In a large skillet, cook bacon over medium heat until crisp. Using a slotted spoon, remove to paper towels to drain, reserving 3 tablespoons drippings. Saute onion and mushrooms in drippings until onion is tender. Stir in the potatoes and soup. Simmer, uncovered, for 5 minutes or until heated through. Sprinkle with bacon.

YIELD: 4 servings.

SAUSAGE, HOMINY AND EGG BRUNCH

MARY ELLEN ANDREWS, NEWVILLE, ALABAMA

PREP: 15 min. BAKE: 30 min.

- 1   pound bulk hot pork sausage
- 6   hard-cooked eggs, sliced
- 2   cans (15 ½ ounces *each*) yellow hominy, drained
- 1   can (10 ¾ ounces) condensed cream of mushroom soup, undiluted
- 1   cup (8 ounces) sour cream
- ¼   teaspoon Worcestershire sauce
- 1   cup (4 ounces) shredded cheddar cheese
- 1   cup soft bread crumbs
- 3   tablespoons butter, melted

In a large skillet, cook sausage over medium heat until no longer pink; drain. Spoon into an ungreased 2½-qt. baking dish. Layer with eggs and hominy. Combine the soup, sour cream and Worcestershire sauce; spread over hominy. Sprinkle with cheese. Combine bread crumbs and butter; sprinkle over top.

Bake, uncovered, at 325° for 30-35 minutes or until bubbly and golden brown. Let stand for 5 minutes before cutting.

YIELD: 6-8 servings.

COOKING TIP

To hard-cook large eggs, place in a single layer in a saucepan and add enough water to cover by 1 in. Cover and bring to a boil. Remove from heat, let stand for 15 minutes. Rinse and place in ice water until cooled.

DO-AHEAD BRUNCH BAKE

JOY MAYNARD, ST. IGNATIUS, MONTANA

PREP: 10 min. + chilling **BAKE:** 80 min. + standing

8	frozen hash brown patties
1	package (8 ounces) thinly sliced fully cooked ham, chopped
1¼	cups shredded reduced-fat cheddar cheese, *divided*
2	cups fat-free milk
1	can (10 ¾ ounces) reduced-fat reduced-sodium condensed cream of mushroom soup, undiluted
1	cup egg substitute
1	teaspoon ground mustard
¼	teaspoon pepper

Place potato patties in a 13-in. x 9-in. x 2-in. baking dish coated with nonstick cooking spray. Top with ham and 1 cup cheese. Combine the milk, soup, egg substitute, mustard and pepper; pour over cheese. Cover and refrigerate overnight.

Remove from the refrigerator 30 minutes before baking. Bake, covered, at 350° for 1 hour. Uncover; sprinkle with remaining cheese. Bake 20-25 minutes longer or until a knife inserted near the center comes out clean. Let stand for 10 minutes before serving.

YIELD: 12 servings.

POTATO EGG SUPPER

ROSEMARY FLEXMAN, WAUKESHA, WISCONSIN

PREP: 20 min. **BAKE:** 30 min.

4	cups diced cooked peeled potatoes
8	bacon strips, cooked and crumbled
4	hard-cooked eggs, sliced
1	can (10 ¾ ounces) condensed cream of mushroom soup, undiluted
½	cup milk
1	small onion, chopped
1	tablespoon chopped green pepper
1	tablespoon chopped sweet red pepper
1	cup (4 ounces) shredded cheddar cheese

Place half of the potatoes in a greased 2-qt. baking dish. Top with the bacon, eggs and remaining potatoes. In a saucepan, combine the soup, milk, onion and peppers. Cook over medium heat until heated through. Pour over the potatoes.

Cover and bake at 350° for 20 minutes. Uncover; sprinkle with cheese. Bake 10-15 minutes longer or until heated through.

YIELD: 4 servings.

SWISS WOODS SOUFFLE

WERNER AND DEBRAH MOSIMANN
LITITZ, PENNSYLVANIA

PREP: 15 min. **BAKE:** 45 min.

8	to 10 slices bread, torn in pieces
5	eggs
2	cups milk, *divided*
1/4	teaspoon salt
1/4	teaspoon pepper
1/2	teaspoon ground mustard
1	pound bulk pork sausage
1	can (10 3/4 ounces) condensed cream of mushroom soup, undiluted *or* 1 cup thick homemade white sauce with 1/2 cup sauteed mushrooms
1	cup (4 ounces) shredded mixed Gruyere and Emmenthaler cheese, *or* aged Swiss

Arrange bread evenly over bottom of 13-in. x 9-in. x 2-in. baking dish. Whisk together the eggs, 1 1/2 cups milk and seasonings; pour over bread and set aside.

In a large skillet, cook sausage over medium heat until no longer pink; drain. Spread meat over bread. Combine the soup, cheese and remaining milk; spread over sausage.

Bake, uncovered, at 350° for about 45 minutes or until brown. Let stand for 5 minutes before serving.

YIELD: 6-8 servings.

SAUSAGE EGG BAKE

MOLLY SWALLOW, BLACKFOOT, IDAHO

PREP: 10 min. **BAKE:** 40 min.

1	pound bulk Italian sausage
2	cans (10 3/4 ounces *each*) condensed cream of potato soup, undiluted
9	eggs
3/4	cup milk
1/4	teaspoon pepper
1	cup (4 ounces) shredded cheddar cheese

In a large skillet, cook sausage over medium heat until no longer pink; drain. Stir in soup. In a mixing bowl, beat the eggs, milk and pepper; stir in sausage mixture.

Transfer to a lightly greased 11-in. x 7-in. x 2-in. baking dish. Sprinkle with cheese. Bake, uncovered, at 375° for 40-45 minutes or until a knife inserted near the center comes out clean. Let stand for 5 minutes before cutting.

YIELD: 12 servings.

OVERNIGHT EGG CASSEROLE

LAVONNE PROPST, SWEET HOME, OREGON

PREP: 15 min. + chilling **BAKE:** 50 min.

- 8   slices bread, cubed
- 3   cups (12 ounces) shredded cheddar cheese
- 1½   pounds bulk pork sausage *or* Italian sausage
- 4   eggs
- 2½   cups milk
- 1   tablespoon prepared mustard
- 1   can (10 ¾ ounces) condensed cream of mushroom soup, undiluted
- ¼   cup chicken broth

Place bread cubes in a greased 13-in. x 9-in. x 2-in. baking dish. Sprinkle with cheese; set aside. In a skillet, cook sausage over medium heat until no longer pink; drain. Crumble sausage over the cheese and bread. Beat the eggs, milk, mustard, soup and broth; pour over sausage. Cover and refrigerate overnight or for at least 2-3 hours before baking.

Remove from the refrigerator 30 minutes before baking. Bake, uncovered, at 350° for 50-60 minutes or just until set. Let stand for 5 minutes before cutting.

YIELD: 6-8 servings.

BACON MUSHROOM BAKE

TAMMI EVANS, BATTLE CREEK, MICHIGAN

PREP: 15 min. **BAKE:** 40 min.

- 18   eggs
- 1½   cups half-and-half cream, *divided*
- 1   can (10 ¾ ounces) condensed cream of chicken soup, undiluted
- ½   pound fresh mushrooms, sliced
- 2   tablespoons butter
- 1   pound sliced bacon, cooked and crumbled
- 2   cups (8 ounces) shredded cheddar cheese

In a large mixing bowl, beat the eggs with 1 cup cream. Pour into a lightly greased large skillet. Cook and stir over medium heat until eggs are set. Combine the soup and remaining cream; set aside.

In another skillet, saute mushrooms in butter until tender. In an ungreased 13-in. x 9-in. x 2-in. baking dish, layer the eggs, bacon, mushrooms and cheese. Pour soup mixture over top.

Bake, uncovered, at 350° for 40 minutes or until heated through. Let stand for 5 minutes before serving.

YIELD: 10-12 servings.

HAM AND POTATO CASSEROLE

ALICE CLARK, QUINCY, FLORIDA

PREP: 15 min. **BAKE:** 35 min.

- 1   package (26 ounces) frozen shredded hash browns
- 3   tablespoons vegetable oil
- 2   cups diced fully cooked ham
- 2   cans (10 ¾ ounces *each*) condensed cream of potato soup, undiluted
- 2   cups (16 ounces) sour cream
- 2   cups (8 ounces) shredded sharp cheddar cheese, *divided*
- ½   cup shredded Parmesan cheese

In a large skillet, fry hash browns in oil until browned. Remove from the heat. Stir in the ham, soup, sour cream, 1½ cups cheddar cheese and Parmesan cheese.

Pour into a greased 13-in. x 9-in. x 2-in. baking dish. Sprinkle with remaining cheddar cheese. Bake, uncovered, at 350° for 30-35 minutes or until heated through.

YIELD: 8-10 servings.

BEEF

VEGGIE MEATBALL MEDLEY (pictured left)

BARBARA KERNOHAN, FOREST, ONTARIO

PREP: 15 min. **COOK:** 20 min.

1	egg, lightly beaten
1/4	cup dry bread crumbs
1/2	teaspoon salt
1/4	teaspoon pepper
1	pound ground beef
2	cups frozen stir-fry vegetable blend
1	medium onion, chopped
1	can (10 3/4 ounces) condensed cream of mushroom soup, undiluted
1/4	cup soy sauce
1/4	teaspoon garlic powder
	Hot cooked rice

In a large bowl, combine the egg, bread crumbs, salt and pepper. Crumble beef over mixture and mix well. Shape into 1 1/2-in. balls.

In a large nonstick skillet, cook meatballs, vegetables and onion until meatballs are browned; drain. Stir in the soup, soy sauce and garlic powder. Bring to a boil. Reduce heat; simmer, uncovered, for 20 minutes or until the meat is no longer pink, stirring occasionally. Serve over rice.

YIELD: 4 servings.

TATER-TOPPED CASSEROLE

VICTORIA MITCHELL, SALEM, VIRGINIA

PREP: 15 min. **BAKE:** 45 min.

1	pound lean ground beef
1/2	cup chopped onion
1/3	cup sliced celery
1/2	teaspoon salt
1/4	teaspoon pepper
1	can (10 3/4 ounces) condensed cream of celery soup, undiluted
1	package (16 ounces) frozen fried potato nuggets
1	cup (4 ounces) shredded cheddar cheese

In a skillet, cook the beef, onion and celery over medium heat until the meat is no longer pink and the vegetables are tender; drain. Stir in salt and pepper.

Spoon mixture into a greased 13-in. x 9-in. x 2-in. baking dish. Spread soup over meat mixture. Top with frozen potatoes. Bake, uncovered, at 400° for about 40 minutes or until bubbly. Sprinkle with cheese. Bake 5 minutes longer or until cheese is melted.

YIELD: 4-6 servings.

Skillet Enchiladas

CATHIE BEARD, PHILOMATH, OREGON

PREP: 10 min. **COOK:** 35 min.

1	pound ground beef
1	medium onion, chopped
1	can (10 ¾ ounces) condensed cream of mushroom soup, undiluted
1	can (10 ounces) enchilada sauce
⅓	cup milk
1	to 2 tablespoons canned chopped green chilies
	Vegetable oil
8	corn tortillas
2 ½	cups (10 ounces) finely shredded cheddar cheese, *divided*
½	cup chopped ripe olives

In a large skillet, cook beef and onion over medium heat until meat is no longer pink; drain. Stir in the soup, enchilada sauce, milk and chilies. Bring to a boil. Reduce heat; cover and simmer for 20 minutes, stirring occasionally.

Meanwhile, in another skillet, heat ¼ in. of oil. Dip each tortilla in hot oil for 3 seconds on each side or just until limp; drain on paper towels. Top each tortilla with ¼ cup cheese and 1 tablespoon olives. Roll up and place over beef mixture, spooning some of mixture over the enchiladas.

Cover and cook until heated through, about 5 minutes. Sprinkle with remaining cheese; cover and cook until cheese is melted.

YIELD: 8 enchiladas.

Meat and Potato Pie

HELEN ELLINGSON, SWAN RIVER, MANITOBA

PREP: 35 min. **BAKE:** 30 min.

2	tablespoons shortening
1 1/2	cups biscuit/baking mix
3	to 4 tablespoons cold water

FILLING:

1 1/2	pounds ground beef
1	medium onion, chopped
1	can (10 3/4 ounces) condensed cream of mushroom soup, undiluted
1/2	teaspoon salt
1/2	teaspoon dried rosemary, crushed
1/2	teaspoon dried thyme
1	can (15 ounces) sliced carrots, drained
1	can (8 ounces) mushroom stems and pieces, drained
2	cups hot mashed potatoes (prepared with milk and butter)
1/2	cup sour cream
1/2	cup shredded cheddar cheese

In a bowl, cut shortening into biscuit mix until the mixture resembles coarse crumbs. Add water, 1 tablespoon at a time, tossing lightly with a fork until dough forms a ball. On a lightly floured surface, roll out pastry to fit a 9-in. pie plate. Line ungreased pie plate with pastry; trim and flute edges or make a decorative edge. Set aside.

In a skillet, cook beef and onion over medium heat until meat is no longer pink; drain. Stir in soup and seasonings; bring to a boil. Reduce heat; simmer, uncovered, for 5 minutes. Pour into pie shell. Top with carrots and mushrooms. Combine potatoes and sour cream; spread over pie.

Bake, uncovered, at 425° for 15 minutes. Reduce heat to 350°. Bake 15 minutes longer or until golden brown. Sprinkle with cheese; let stand for 5-10 minutes.

YIELD: 6 servings.

Different Pizza

CARLA WIESE, RIPON, WISCONSIN

PREP: 15 min. **BAKE:** 25 min.

1	pound ground beef
1/3	cup chopped onion
2	teaspoons Worcestershire sauce
1/2	teaspoon dried marjoram
1/2	teaspoon dried oregano
1/4	teaspoon dried sage
1/4	teaspoon pepper
1	can (10 3/4 ounces) condensed cream of mushroom soup, undiluted

CRUST:

2	cups all-purpose flour
2	teaspoons baking powder
1/2	teaspoon salt
1/4	cup shortening
1	cup milk
2	cups (8 ounces) shredded part-skim mozzarella cheese

In a large skillet, cook beef and onion over medium heat until no longer pink; drain well. Stir in the Worcestershire sauce, marjoram, oregano, sage, pepper and soup. Stir until well blended; set aside.

For crust, in a bowl, combine the flour, baking powder and salt; cut in shortening. Add milk and stir until combined (mixture resembles a soft biscuit dough). Pat dough into a lightly greased 15-in. x 10-in. x 1-in. baking pan.

Spread beef mixture over crust. Sprinkle with mozzarella cheese. Bake at 400° for 25 to 30 minutes or until lightly browned.

YIELD: 16 servings.

COUNTRY-FRIED STEAK

BETTY CLAYCOMB, ALVERTON, PENNSYLVANIA

PREP/TOTAL TIME: 20 min.

1/2	cup all-purpose flour
1/2	teaspoon salt
1/2	teaspoon pepper
3/4	cup buttermilk
1	cup crushed saltines (about 30 crackers)
4	beef cube steaks (1 pound)
3	tablespoons vegetable oil
1	can (10 3/4 ounces) condensed cream of mushrooms soup, undiluted
1	cup milk

In a shallow bowl, combine the flour, salt and pepper. Place buttermilk in another shallow bowl and the saltine crumbs in a third bowl. Coat steaks with flour mixture, then dip into buttermilk and coat with crumbs.

In a large skillet, cook steaks in hot oil over medium-high heat for 2-3 minutes on each side or until golden and no longer pink. Remove and keep warm.

Add soup and milk to skillet; bring to a boil, stirring to loosen browned bits from pan. Serve gravy with steaks.

YIELD: 4 servings.

ZIPPY BEEF SUPPER

RUTH FOSTER, CROOKSVILLE, OHIO

PREP: 15 min. BAKE: 35 min.

2	pounds ground beef
1	medium onion, chopped
1	cup cubed cooked potatoes
1	can (11 ounces) condensed nacho cheese soup, undiluted
1	can (10 3/4 ounces) condensed cream of onion soup, undiluted
1	can (10 ounces) diced tomatoes and green chilies, undrained
2	to 3 teaspoons ground cumin
1/2	to 1 teaspoon garlic powder
3	cups crushed tortilla chips
1	cup (4 ounces) shredded cheddar cheese

In a large saucepan, cook beef and onion over medium heat until meat is no longer pink; drain. Add potatoes; cook and stir until heated through. Stir in the soups, tomatoes, cumin and garlic powder; mix well.

Transfer to a greased 13-in. x 9-in. x 2-in. baking dish. Cover and bake at 350° for 30 minutes. Uncover; sprinkle with tortilla chips and cheese. Bake 5-10 minutes longer or until cheese is melted.

YIELD: 6-8 servings.

COOKING TIP

For added zip in ZIPPY BEEF SUPPER, use 1 cup shredded pepper Jack cheese for the cheddar cheese.

POPULAR POTLUCK CASSEROLE

DEBBI SMITH, CROSSETT, ARKANSAS

PREP: 25 min. **BAKE:** 25 min.

- 1   package (7 ounces) shell macaroni
- 2   pounds ground beef
- 1   medium onion, chopped
- ¼   cup chopped green pepper
- ¼   cup thinly sliced celery
- 1   can (10 ¾ ounces) condensed cream of mushroom soup, undiluted
- 1   can (10 ounces) diced tomatoes with green chilies
- 1   can (8 ounces) tomato sauce
- 1   to 2 tablespoons chili powder
- 1   can (15 ¾ ounces) whole kernel corn, drained
- 2   cups (8 ounces) shredded cheddar cheese, *divided*

Cook macaroni according to package directions. Meanwhile, in a large skillet, cook the beef, onion, green pepper and celery until meat is no longer pink and vegetables are tender; drain. Stir in the soup, tomatoes, tomato sauce and chili powder; mix well. Drain the macaroni; stir into beef mixture. Add the corn and 1½ cups cheese.

Transfer to a greased 13-in. x 9-in. x 2-in. baking dish. Sprinkle with remaining cheese. Bake, uncovered, at 350° for 25-30 minutes or until heated through.

YIELD: 10-12 servings.

SAVE A PENNY CASSEROLE

JANICE MILLER, WORTHINGTON, KENTUCKY

PREP: 10 min. **BAKE:** 30 min.

- 1   pound ground beef
- 1   can (10 ¾ ounces) condensed cream of mushroom soup, undiluted
- 1   can (14 ¾ ounces) spaghetti in tomato-cheese sauce
- 1   can (15 to 16 ounces) mixed vegetables, drained
- 1   cup (4 ounces) shredded cheddar cheese, optional

In a skillet, cook beef over medium heat until no longer pink; drain. Stir in the soup, spaghetti and vegetables.

Transfer to an ungreased 11-in. x 7-in. x 2-in. baking dish. Bake, uncovered, at 350° for 30 minutes or until heated through. If desired, sprinkle with cheese and let stand a few minutes until melted.

YIELD: 4-6 servings.

ROUND STEAK 'N' DUMPLINGS

FANCHEON RESLER, GOSHEN, INDIANA

PREP: 45 min. **BAKE:** 25 min.

- 1/3 cup all-purpose flour
- 1 teaspoon paprika
- 2 pounds boneless beef round steak, cut into 1/2-inch cubes
- 2 cups frozen pearl onions, thawed
- 1/4 cup vegetable oil
- 2 1/2 cups water
- 1/2 teaspoon salt
- 1/4 teaspoon pepper
- 1 can (10 3/4 ounces) condensed cream of mushroom soup, undiluted
- 2 jars (4 1/2 ounces *each*) whole mushrooms, drained

DUMPLINGS:
- 2 cups all-purpose flour
- 4 teaspoons baking powder
- 1 teaspoon dried minced onion
- 1 teaspoon celery seed
- 1 teaspoon poultry seasoning
- 1/2 teaspoon salt
- 1/2 teaspoon rubbed sage
- 1 cup milk
- 1/4 cup vegetable oil
- 1 1/2 cups soft bread crumbs
- 1/4 cup butter, melted

In a large resealable plastic bag, combine the flour and paprika; add beef in batches and shake to coat. In a Dutch oven, cook beef and onions in oil over medium heat until meat is no longer pink. Add the water, salt and pepper; bring to a boil. Reduce heat; cover and simmer for 35-45 minutes. Stir in soup and mushrooms.

For dumplings, combine the first seven ingredients in a bowl. Stir in milk and oil just until moistened. In a shallow dish, combine bread crumbs and butter. Drop heaping tablespoonfuls of dumpling batter into crumb mixture; turn to coat. Transfer hot beef mixture to a greased 2 1/2-qt. baking dish. Top with dumplings.

Bake, uncovered, at 425° for 25-30 minutes or until bubbly and golden brown and a toothpick inserted in dumplings comes out clean.

YIELD: **8 servings.**

POTATO SLOPPY JOE BAKE

RUTH CHIARENZA, LA VALE, MARYLAND

PREP: 15 min. **BAKE:** 20 min.

- 1 pound ground beef
- 1 can (15 1/2 ounces) sloppy joe sauce
- 1 can (10 3/4 ounces) condensed cream of potato soup, undiluted
- 1 package (32 ounces) frozen cubed hash brown potatoes, thawed
- 1 cup (4 ounces) shredded cheddar cheese

In a skillet, cook beef over medium heat until no longer pink; drain. Add sloppy joe sauce and soup. Place hash browns in a greased 13-in. x 9-in. x 2-in. baking dish. Top with beef mixture.

Cover and bake at 450° for 20 minutes. Uncover; bake 10 minutes longer or until heated through. Sprinkle with cheese.

YIELD: **6-8 servings.**

COUNTRY GOULASH SKILLET

LISA NEUBERT, SOUTH OGDEN, UTAH

PREP: 15 min. **COOK:** 20 min.

- 1   pound ground beef
- 1   can (28 ounces) stewed tomatoes
- 1   can (10 ¾ ounces) condensed cream of mushroom soup, undiluted
- 2   cups fresh *or* frozen corn
- 1   medium green pepper, chopped
- 1   medium onion, chopped
- 1   tablespoon Worcestershire sauce
- 3   cups cooked elbow macaroni

In a large skillet, cook beef over medium heat until no longer pink; drain. Stir in the tomatoes, soup, corn, green pepper, onion and Worcestershire sauce. Bring to a boil. Reduce heat; cover and simmer for 20-25 minutes or until vegetables are tender. Stir in macaroni and heat through.

YIELD: 6-8 servings.

QUICK MUSHROOM STEW

CHERIE SECHRIST, RED LION, PENNSYLVANIA

PREP: 10 min. **BAKE:** 2 1/2 hours

1	can (10 3/4 ounces) condensed tomato soup, undiluted
1	can (10 3/4 ounces) condensed cream of mushroom soup, undiluted
2 1/2	cups water
2	pounds beef stew meat, cut into cubes
2	bay leaves
3	medium potatoes, peeled and cut into 1-inch chunks
4	carrots, cut into 1/2-inch slices
1	pound medium fresh mushrooms, halved
1	tablespoon quick-cooking tapioca

In a Dutch oven, combine the soups and water until smooth. Add meat and bay leaves. Cover and bake at 325° for 1 1/2 hours.

Stir in the potatoes, carrots, mushrooms and tapioca. Cover and bake 1 hour longer or until the meat and vegetables are tender. Discard the bay leaves before serving.

YIELD: 6-8 servings.

HOME-STYLE COOKING WITH CREAM SOUP | **BEEF**

BACON NUT MEATBALLS

SUE DOWNES-WILLIAMS, LEBANON, NEW HAMPSHIRE

PREP: 25 min. **COOK:** 30 min.

10	bacon strips, diced
2	eggs
1/3	cup tomato paste
1 1/2	cups soft bread crumbs
1/3	cup minced fresh parsley
2	tablespoons chopped slivered almonds
1	tablespoon dried oregano
1	tablespoon salt
1 1/2	teaspoons pepper
2	pounds ground beef
1	pound fresh mushrooms, sliced
1	medium onion, chopped
2	cans (10 3/4 ounces *each*) condensed cream of mushrooom soup, undiluted
1	can (10 1/2 ounces) beef consomme

In a large skillet, cook bacon over medium heat until crisp. Using a slotted spoon, remove to paper towels; drain, reserving drippings.

In a large bowl, combine the eggs, tomato paste, crumbs, parsley, almonds, oregano, salt, pepper and bacon. Crumble beef over mixture and mix well. Shape into 1-in. balls. Brown meatballs in drippings. Remove with a slotted spoon. Drain, reserving 1 tablespoon drippings.

Saute mushrooms and onion in the drippings. Combine soup and consomme; stir into the mushroom mixture until blended. Return meatballs to pan. Bring to a boil. Reduce heat; simmer, uncovered, for 10 minutes or until meat is no longer pink.

YIELD: 60 meatballs.

THREE-STEP STROGANOFF

JOYCE KEY, SNELLVILLE, GEORGIA

PREP/TOTAL TIME: 30 min.

1 1/2	pounds boneless beef round steak, thinly sliced
1	tablespoon vegetable oil
1	can (10 3/4 ounces) condensed cream of mushroom soup, undiluted
1/2	cup water
1	envelope onion soup mix
1/2	cup sour cream
	Hot cooked noodles
	Minced fresh parsley, optional

In a large skillet, stir-fry beef in oil until no longer pink. Stir in the soup, water and onion soup mix.

Reduce heat; cover and simmer for 20 minutes. Stir in sour cream; heat through (do not boil). Serve over noodles; garnish with parsley if desired.

YIELD: 6 servings.

COMPANY CASSEROLE

EDNA DAVIS, DENVER, COLORADO

PREP: 30 min. **BAKE:** 20 min.

2	pounds lean ground beef
1/2	cup sour cream
3	tablespoons dry onion soup mix
1	egg, beaten
1 1/2	cups soft bread crumbs
1/4	cup butter
1	can (8 ounces) mushroom stems and pieces, undrained
1	can (10 3/4 ounces) condensed cream of chicken soup, undiluted
1 2/3	cups water

SAUCE: (optional)

1	can (10 3/4 ounces) condensed cream of chicken soup, undiluted
1/4	teaspoon poultry seasoning
1	teaspoon dried minced onion
1/2	cup sour cream

BUTTER CRUMB DUMPLINGS:

2	cups all-purpose flour
4	teaspoons baking powder
1	tablespoon poppy seeds
1	teaspoon celery salt
1	teaspoon poultry seasoning
2	teaspoons dried minced onion
1/4	cup vegetable oil
3/4	cup plus 2 tablespoons milk
1/4	cup butter, melted
2	cups soft bread crumbs

In a mixing bowl, combine first five ingredients. Shape into 16 balls. In a large skillet; brown meatballs in butter over medium-low heat. Stir in the mushrooms, soup and water. Bring to a boil. Reduce heat; simmer, uncovered for 20 minutes, adding more water if necessary.

Transfer to a 3-qt. baking dish. If extra sauce is desired, combine the cream of chicken soup, poultry seasoning and minced onion in a small saucepan. Cook until heated through. Remove from heat and stir in sour cream; pour over meatball mixture.

For dumplings, in a bowl, combine the flour, baking powder, poppy seeds, celery salt, poultry seasoning and onion. Stir in oil and milk. Combine butter and bread crumbs. Drop heaping tablespoonful of dough into buttered crumbs; roll to coat evenly. Cover meatball mixture with dumplings.

Bake at 400°, uncovered, for 20 to 25 minutes or until dumplings are golden and a toothpick inserted near the center comes out clean.

YIELD: 4-6 servings.

CLASSIC POT ROAST

JAN ROAT, GRASS RANGE, MONTANA

PREP: 15 min. **BAKE:** 1 1/2 hours

1	boneless beef sirloin tip *or* 1 beef bottom round roast (about 2 pounds)
2	medium potatoes, cut into chunks
2	medium carrots, cut into 2-inch chunks
1	medium onion, cut into wedges
1/4	teaspoon pepper
1	can (14 1/2 ounces) Italian stewed tomatoes, undrained
1	can (10 3/4 ounces) condensed cream of mushroom soup, undiluted
1/2	cup water

Place meat in an ovenproof skillet or Dutch oven. Add the potatoes, carrots and onion. Sprinkle with pepper. Top with tomatoes. Spread soup over meat. Pour water around vegetables.

Cover and bake at 325° for 1 1/2 hours or until meat and vegetables are tender. Thicken cooking liquid if desired.

YIELD: 6-8 servings.

MASHED POTATO HOT DISH

TANYA ABERNATHY, YACOLT, WASHINGTON

PREP: 15 min. **BAKE:** 20 min.

- 1 pound ground beef
- 1 can (10 ¾ ounces) condensed cream of chicken soup, undiluted
- 2 cups frozen French-style green beans
- 2 cups hot mashed potatoes (prepared with milk and butter)
- ½ cup shredded cheddar cheese

In a large skillet, cook beef over medium heat until no longer pink; drain. Stir in soup and beans.

Transfer to a greased 2-qt. baking dish. Top with mashed potatoes; sprinkle with cheese. Bake, uncovered, at 350° for 20-25 minutes or until heated through and cheese is melted.

YIELD: 4 servings.

COOKING TIP

About 1 ¼ pounds of potatoes will yield a generous 2 cups mashed potatoes.

MEXICAN CHIP CASSEROLE

DORIS HEATH, FRANKLIN, NORTH CAROLINA

PREP/TOTAL TIME: 20 min.

- 1   pound ground beef
- 1   medium onion, chopped
- 1   garlic clove, minced
- 1   can (10 3/4 ounces) condensed cream of mushroom soup, undiluted
- 1   can (11 ounces) Mexicorn, drained
- 1   can (4 ounces) chopped green chilies, drained
- 1   package (10 1/2 ounces) corn chips
- 1   can (10 ounces) enchilada sauce
- 1   to 2 cups (4 to 8 ounces) shredded Co-Jack cheese

In a skillet, cook the beef, onion and garlic over medium heat until meat is no longer; drain. Add the soup, corn and chilies; mix well.

In an ungreased shallow 3-qt. baking dish, layer the meat mixture, corn chips and enchilada sauce; top with cheese. Bake, uncovered, at 350° for 8-10 minutes or until heated through.

YIELD: 6 servings.

MEATBALLS WITH MUSHROOM SAUCE

JOYCE WATSON, PIGGOTT, ARKANSAS

PREP: 20 min. BAKE: 30 min.

- 1/4   cup evaporated milk
- 1/4   cup dry bread crumbs
- 1/2   teaspoon salt
- 1/4   teaspoon pepper
- 1 1/2   pounds ground beef

SAUCE:

- 1   can (10 3/4 ounces) condensed cream of mushroom soup, undiluted
- 2/3   cup evaporated milk
- 2/3   cup water

In a large bowl, combine the first four ingredients. Crumble beef over mixture and mix well. Shape into 1 1/2-in. balls. In a large ovenproof skillet, brown meatballs; drain.

Combine sauce ingredients; pour over the meatballs. Bake, uncovered, at 350° for 30-35 minutes or until meat is no longer pink.

YIELD: 30 meatballs.

COOKING TIP

You can also use seasoned bread crumbs in the meatball mixture above.

SAUERKRAUT HOT DISH

LUCY MOHLMAN, CRETE, NEBRASKA

PREP: 15 min. **BAKE:** 45 min.

1	pound ground beef
1/4	cup chopped onion
1/2	teaspoon salt
1/2	teaspoon pepper
1	can (32 ounces) sauerkraut, drained
2	cups uncooked egg noodles
1	can (10 3/4 ounces) condensed cream of celery soup, undiluted
1	can (10 3/4 ounces) condensed cream of mushroom soup, undiluted
1	cup milk
1	to 1 1/2 cups (4 to 6 ounces) shredded cheddar cheese

In a skillet, cook the beef, onion, salt and pepper over medium heat until meat is no longer pink; drain. Spoon half of the ground beef mixture into a 13-in. x 9-in. x 2-in. baking dish. Top with half of the sauerkraut and half of the noodles. Repeat layers. Combine soups and milk; pour over noodles.

Cover and bake at 350° for 30 minutes. Uncover; sprinkle with cheese. Bake 15 to 20 minutes longer or until heated through.

YIELD: 4-6 servings.

CREAMY CORNED BEEF BAKE

BRENDA MYERS, OVERLAND PARK, KANSAS

PREP: 20 min. **BAKE:** 40 min. + standing

1	package (7 ounces) small shell pasta
1 1/2	cups cubed cooked corned beef *or* 1 can (12 ounces) cooked corned beef
1	can (10 3/4 ounces) condensed cream of chicken soup, undiluted
8	ounces cheddar cheese, cubed
1	cup milk
1/2	cup chopped onion
2	bread slices, cubed
2	tablespoons butter, melted

Cook pasta according to package directions; drain. In a bowl, combine the pasta, corned beef, soup, cheese, milk and onion.

Transfer to a greased 2-qt. baking dish. Toss bread cubes with butter; sprinkle over top. Bake, uncovered, at 350° for 40-45 minutes or until golden brown. Let stand for 10 minutes before serving.

YIELD: 4 servings.

Beef and Noodle Casserole

MARY HINMAN, ESCONDIDO, CALIFORNIA

PREP: 20 min. **BAKE:** 45 min.

1	package (10 ounces) wide noodles
1½	pounds ground beef
1	large onion, chopped
1	cup chopped green pepper
1	tablespoon butter
1	tablespoon Worcestershire sauce
2	cans (10 ¾ ounces *each*) condensed cream of tomato soup, undiluted
1	can (10 ¾ ounces) cream of mushroom soup, undiluted
1	cup (4 ounces) shredded cheddar cheese

Cook noodles according to package directions. In a large skillet, cook beef over medium heat until no longer pink. Drain beef and set aside.

In the same skillet, saute onion and pepper in butter until tender. Drain noodles; add to skillet along with the Worcestershire sauce, soups and reserved beef; mix well.

Spoon into a greased 3-qt. baking dish; top with cheese. Bake at 350° for 45 minutes or until heated through.

YIELD: 8 servings.

Meaty Chili Lasagna

MELBA NESMITH, CORSICANA, TEXAS

PREP: 20 min. **BAKE:** 45 min. + standing

12	uncooked lasagna noodles
1 ½	pounds ground beef
1	medium onion, chopped
1	medium green pepper, chopped
2	to 3 jalapeno peppers, seeded and chopped
1	to 2 tablespoons chili powder
1	garlic clove, minced
1	can (10 ¾ ounces) condensed cream of mushroom soup, undiluted
1	cup frozen corn
1	can (8 ounces) tomato sauce
3	tablespoons tomato paste
1	can (2 ¼ ounces) sliced ripe olives, drained
4	cups (16 ounces) shredded cheddar cheese

Cook noodles according to package directions. Meanwhile, in a large skillet, cook the beef, onion, peppers, chili powder and garlic over medium heat until meat is no longer pink; drain. Add the soup, corn, tomato sauce, tomato paste and olives; simmer until heated through.

Drain noodles. Spread ½ cup meat sauce in a greased 13-in. x 9-in. x 2-in. baking dish. Layer with four noodles, half of the remaining sauce and 1 ⅓ cups cheese. Repeat layers once. Top with remaining noodles and cheese.

Cover and bake at 350° for 30 minutes. Uncover; bake 15 minutes longer or until cheese is melted. Let stand for 15 minutes before cutting.

YIELD: 12 servings.

EDITOR'S NOTE: When cutting or seeding hot peppers, use rubber or plastic gloves to protect your hands. Avoid touching your face.

Country Meat Loaf

JIM HOPKINS, WHITTIER, CALIFORNIA

PREP: 10 min. **BAKE:** 1 ½ hours

2	eggs, lightly beaten
1	can (10 ¾ ounces) condensed cream of celery soup, undiluted
½	teaspoon pepper
1	package (6 ounces) corn bread stuffing mix
1 ½	pounds ground beef
½	pound ground veal
¼	pound ground pork

In a large bowl, combine the eggs, soup, pepper and stuffing mix. Crumble the beef, veal and pork over the stuffing mixture and mix well.

Press into a 9-in. x 5-in. x 3-in. loaf pan. Bake at 350° for 1 ½ hours or until a thermometer reads 160°. Drain.

YIELD: 6-8 servings.

Easy Skillet Supper

LARUE FLAA, WAHPETON, NORTH DAKOTA

PREP: 15 min. **COOK:** 45 min.

1	pound lean ground beef
4	medium potatoes, peeled and diced
2	cups fresh *or* frozen corn
1	small onion, chopped
	Salt and pepper to taste
1	can (10 ¾ ounces) condensed cream of mushroom soup, undiluted

In a skillet, crumble beef. Top with the potatoes, corn and onion. Sprinkle with salt and pepper. Spread soup over top.

Cover and cook over medium heat for 10 minutes. Reduce heat; cover and simmer for 30-45 minutes or until meat is no longer pink and potatoes are tender.

YIELD: 4-6 servings.

STEAK ROLL-UPS

PAT HABIGER, SPEARVILLE, KANSAS

PREP: 20 min. **COOK:** 2 hours

1 1/2	pounds boneless round steak
1/4	cup chopped onion
1/4	cup butter, melted
2	cups fresh bread cubes
1/2	cup chopped celery
1	tablespoon dried parsley flakes
1/2	teaspoon salt
1/2	teaspoon poultry seasoning
1/4	teaspoon pepper
1	cup all-purpose flour
2	tablespoons vegetable oil
1	can (10 3/4 ounces) condensed cream of mushroom soup, undiluted
1 1/3	cups water
3/4	teaspoon browning sauce, optional

Pound steak to 1/3-in. thickness. Cut into six pieces. Combine the onion, butter, bread cubes, celery and seasonings. Place 1/3 cup on each piece of steak; roll up and fasten with a toothpick. Roll in flour.

In a large skillet, brown roll-ups in oil. Combine the soup, water and browning sauce if desired; pour over roll-ups. Bring to a boil. Reduce heat; cover and simmer for 2 hours or until meat is tender, turning occasionally.

YIELD: 6 servings.

CHEESY BEEF MACARONI

DENA EVETTS, SENTINEL, OKLAHOMA

PREP: 25 min. **BAKE:** 20 min.

1	pound ground beef
1	can (15 1/4 ounces) whole kernel corn, drained
1	can (10 3/4 ounces) condensed cream of chicken soup, undiluted
8	ounces process cheese (Velveeta), shredded
2 1/2	cups cooked elbow macaroni

In a large skillet, cook beef over medium heat until no longer pink; drain. Add the corn and soup. Set aside 1/2 cup cheese for topping; stir remaining cheese into meat mixture until melted. Gently stir in macaroni until coated.

Transfer to a greased 8-in. square baking dish. Top with reserved cheese. Bake, uncovered, at 350° for 20-25 minutes or until heated through.

YIELD: 4-6 servings.

SHEPHERD'S PIE

VALERIE MERRILL, TOPEKA, KANSAS

PREP: 20 min. **BAKE:** 30 min.

2 1/2	pounds potatoes, peeled and cooked
1	to 1 1/2 cups (8 to 12 ounces) sour cream
	Salt and pepper to taste
2	pounds ground beef
1/2	cup chopped onion
1	medium sweet red pepper, chopped
1	teaspoon garlic salt
1	can (10 3/4 ounces) condensed cream of mushroom soup, undiluted
1	can (16 ounces) whole kernel corn, drained
1/2	cup milk
2	tablespoons butter, melted
	Chopped fresh parsley, optional

Mash potatoes with sour cream. Add salt and pepper; set aside. In a skillet, cook the beef, onion and red pepper over medium heat until meat is no longer pink and vegetables are tender; drain. Stir in garlic salt. Add the soup, corn and milk; mix well.

Spread meat mixture into a shallow 3-qt. baking dish. Top with mashed potatoes; drizzle with butter.

Bake, uncovered, at 350° for 30 to 35 minutes or until heated through. For additional browning, place under broiler for a few minutes. Sprinkle with parsley if desired.

YIELD: 8-10 servings.

In a large skillet, brown the patties in oil; drain. Combine the remaining soup mixture with water; pour over patties. Cover and cook over low heat for 10-15 minutes or until meat is done. Remove patties to a serving platter; spoon sauce over meat. Sprinkle with parsley.

YIELD: 6 servings.

CABBAGE CASSEROLE

NANCY MATHIOWETZ, HECTOR, MINNESOTA

PREP: 25 min. **BAKE:** 1 1/2 hours

5	cups shredded cabbage
6	medium potatoes, sliced
4	medium carrots, sliced
1	small onion, chopped
1	teaspoon salt
1/2	teaspoon pepper
1	pound lean ground beef
1	can (10 3/4 ounces) condensed cream of mushroom soup, undiluted
1	can (10 1/2 ounces) condensed vegetable beef soup, undiluted

In a bowl, combine the first six ingredients; mix well. Crumble beef over mixture; toss gently.

Transfer to a greased 3-qt. baking dish. Spread soups over top. Cover and bake at 350° for 1 1/2 hours or until the meat is no longer pink and the vegetables are tender.

YIELD: 10 servings.

SALISBURY STEAK DELUXE

DENISE BARTEET, SHREVEPORT, LOUISIANA

PREP/TOTAL TIME: 30 min.

1	can (10 3/4 ounces) condensed cream of mushroom soup, undiluted
1	tablespoon prepared mustard
2	teaspoons Worcestershire sauce
1	teaspoon prepared horseradish
1	egg, lightly beaten
1/4	cup dry bread crumbs
1/4	cup finely chopped onion
1/2	teaspoon salt
	Dash pepper
1 1/2	pound ground beef
1	to 2 tablespoons vegetable oil
1/2	cup water
2	tablespoons chopped fresh parsley

In a bowl, combine the soup, mustard, Worcestershire sauce and horseradish; set aside. In another bowl, combine the egg, bread crumbs, onion, salt, pepper and 1/4 cup of the soup mixture. Crumble beef over mixture and mix well. Shape into six patties.

COOKING TIP

If you're in a hurry, use 5 cups of cabbage coleslaw mix for the shredded cabbage.

MEAT-AND-POTATO CASSEROLE

MARNA HEITZ, FARLEY, IOWA

PREP: 10 min. **BAKE:** 45 min.

- 3 to 4 cups thinly sliced peeled potatoes
- 2 tablespoons butter, melted
- 1/2 teaspoon salt
- 1 pound ground beef
- 1 package (10 ounces) frozen corn, thawed
- 1 can (10 3/4 ounces) condensed cream of celery soup, undiluted
- 1/3 cup milk
- 1/4 teaspoon garlic powder
- 1/8 teaspoon pepper
- 1 tablespoon chopped onion
- 1 cup (4 ounces) shredded cheddar cheese, *divided*

    Snipped fresh parsley, optional

Toss potatoes with butter and salt; arrange on the bottom and up the sides of a greased 13-in. x 9-in. x 2-in. baking dish. Bake, uncovered, at 400° for 25 to 30 minutes or until potatoes are almost tender.

Meanwhile, in a skillet, cook beef over medium heat until no longer pink; drain. Sprinkle beef and corn over potatoes. Combine the soup, milk, garlic powder, pepper, onion and 1/2 cup cheese; pour over beef mixture.

Bake, uncovered, at 400° for 20 minutes or until vegetables are tender. Top with remaining cheese. Bake 2 to 3 minutes longer or until the cheese is melted. Garnish with parsley if desired.

YIELD: 6 servings.

HAMBURGER STROGANOFF

JUTTA DOERING, KELOWNA, BRITISH COLUMBIA

PREP/TOTAL TIME: 30 min.

1 1/2	pounds lean ground beef
1/2	cup chopped onion
2	tablespoons butter
2	tablespoons all-purpose flour
1/2	teaspoon salt
1	garlic clove, minced
1/4	teaspoon pepper
1	can (4 ounce) mushroom pieces and stems, drained
1	can (10 3/4 ounces) condensed cream of chicken soup, undiluted
1	cup (8 ounces) sour cream

POPPY SEED NOODLES:

8	ounces wide noodles, cooked and drained
2	teaspoons poppy seeds
1	tablespoon butter, melted
	Chopped fresh parsley

In a skillet, cook ground beef in onion and butter over medium heat until the meat is no longer pink; drain. Stir in the flour, salt, garlic, pepper and mushrooms. Cook for 5 minutes, stirring constantly.

Stir in soup; bring to a boil, stirring constantly. Reduce heat; simmer, uncovered, for 10 minutes, stirring occasionally. Stir in sour cream; heat through (do not boil).

Meanwhile, combine the noodles, poppy seeds and butter; toss lightly. Spoon stroganoff over noodles. Garnish with parsley.

YIELD: 6 servings.

POTATO BEEF CASSEROLE

SANDRA JONGS, ABBOTSFORD, BRITISH COLUMBIA

PREP: 20 min. **BAKE:** 70 min.

1	pound ground beef
1/2	cup chopped onion
1/2	cup chopped celery
2	tablespoons chopped celery leaves
1	can (10 3/4 ounces) condensed cream of mushroom soup, undiluted
1/2	cup milk
1	teaspoon Worcestershire sauce
1/2	teaspoon pepper
4	medium potatoes, peeled and thinly sliced
1	teaspoon salt, optional

In a skillet, cook the beef, onion, celery and celery leaves over medium heat until meat is no longer pink and vegetables are tender; drain. Remove from the heat; stir in soup, milk, Worcestershire sauce and pepper.

Place half of the potatoes in a greased 2-qt. baking dish; sprinkle with 1/2 teaspoon salt if desired. Top with half of the beef mixture. Repeat layers. Cover and bake at 400° for 1 hour and 10 minutes or until the potatoes are tender.

YIELD: 4 servings.

DIJON MUSHROOM BEEF

JUDITH MCGHAN, PERRY HALL, MARYLAND

PREP/TOTAL TIME: 20 min.

1/2	pound fresh mushrooms, sliced
1	medium onion, sliced
2	teaspoons olive oil
1	pound boneless beef sirloin steak, thinly sliced
1	can (10 3/4 ounces) reduced-fat reduced-sodium condensed cream of mushroom soup, undiluted
3/4	cup fat-free milk
2	tablespoons Dijon mustard
	Hot cooked yolk-free noodles, optional

In a large nonstick skillet, saute mushrooms and onion in oil until tender. Remove and set aside.

In the same skillet, cook beef over medium heat until no longer pink. Add the soup, milk, mustard and mushroom mixture. Bring to a boil. Reduce heat; cook and stir until thickened. Serve over hot cooked noodles if desired.

YIELD: 4 servings.

CANDLELIGHT STEW

GERTIE BROOKS, ALMONT, MICHIGAN

PREP: 10 min. **BAKE:** 2 hours

2	pounds beef stew meat
2	tablespoons vegetable oil
	Salt and pepper
1	can (10 ¾ ounces) condensed cream of mushroom soup
1	medium carrot, shredded
⅓	cup burgundy wine *or* beef broth
1	can (8 ounces) sliced mushrooms, drained *or* ½ pound fresh
2	tablespoons dry onion soup mix

In a large skillet, brown meat in hot oil in batches; sprinkle with salt and pepper. Transfer to 2-qt. baking dish. Combine remaining ingredients; pour over meat.

Cover and bake at 350° for 2 hours or until meat is tender. Stir stew occasionally as it bakes. Add small amount of beef broth if you like more gravy.

YIELD: 6 servings.

ROUND STEAK SUPPER

SANDRA CASTILLO, JANESVILLE, WISCONSIN

PREP: 5 min. **COOK:** 6 hours

4	large potatoes, peeled and cut into ½-inch cubes
1½	pounds boneless beef round steak
1	can (10 ¾ ounces) condensed cream of mushroom soup, undiluted
½	cup water
1	envelope onion soup mix
	Pepper and garlic powder to taste

Place the potatoes into a 3-qt. slow cooker. Cut beef into four pieces; place over potatoes. In a bowl, combine the soup, water, soup mix, pepper and garlic powder. Pour over the beef. Cover and cook on low for 6-8 hours or until meat and potatoes are tender.

YIELD: 4 servings.

SWEDISH MEATBALLS

RUTH ANDREWSON, LEAVENWORTH, WASHINGTON

PREP: 30 min. **BAKE:** 45 min.

1	egg, lightly beaten
½	cup milk
¾	cup dry bread crumbs
¾	cup finely chopped onion
1	teaspoon Worcestershire sauce
1	teaspoon salt
½	to ¾ teaspoon ground allspice
¼	teaspoon pepper
1½	pounds ground beef
¾	pound ground pork
1	tablespoon vegetable oil
1	can (10 ¾ ounces) condensed cream of mushroom soup, undiluted
½	cup water
	Hot cooked noodles

In a bowl, combine the egg, milk, bread crumbs, onion, Worcestershire sauce and seasonings. Crumble meat over mixture and mix well. Shape into 1½-in. balls. In a large skillet, brown meatballs in oil in small batches over medium heat; drain.

Place meatballs in a greased 2-qt. baking dish. Combine the soup and water; pour over the meatballs. Bake, uncovered, at 350° for about 40-45 minutes or until the meat is no longer pink. Serve over egg noodles.

YIELD: 10 servings.

BAKED SPAGHETTI

RUTH KOBERNA, BRECKSVILLE, OHIO

PREP: 20 min. **BAKE:** 30 min.

12	ounces spaghetti
1	pound ground beef
1	cup chopped onion
1	cup chopped green pepper
1	tablespoon butter
1	can (28 ounces) diced tomatoes, undrained
1	can (4 ounces) mushroom stems and pieces, drained
1	can (2 1/4 ounces) sliced ripe olives, drained
2	teaspoons dried oregano
2	cups (8 ounces) shredded cheddar cheese
1	can (10 3/4 ounces) condensed cream of mushroom soup, undiluted
1/4	cup water
1/4	cup grated Parmesan cheese

Cook pasta according to package directions. Meanwhile, in a large skillet, cook beef over medium heat until no longer pink. Drain and set aside. In same skillet, saute onion and green pepper in butter until tender. Add the tomatoes, mushrooms, olives, oregano and reserved ground beef. Simmer, uncovered, for 10 minutes.

Drain pasta and place half in a greased 13-in. x 9-in. x 2-in. baking dish. Top with half of the beef mixture. Sprinkle with 1 cup cheddar cheese. Repeat layers.

Mix the soup and water until smooth; pour over casserole. Sprinkle with Parmesan cheese. Bake, uncovered, at 350° for 30-35 minutes or until heated through.

YIELD: 12 servings.

1 teaspoon celery salt
Pepper to taste
1 large onion, sliced ¼ inch thick
8 bacon strips
¼ cup butter, cubed

Place roast in a large roasting pan fat side up. Combine the broth, gravy, soup, water, Worcestershire sauce and soy sauce; pour over roast. Sprinkle with seasonings. Arrange onion slices over roast. Place bacon strips diagonally over onion. Dot with butter.

Bake, uncovered, at 325° for 2½ to 3½ hours or until the meat reaches desired doneness (for medium-rare, a meat thermometer should read 145°; medium, 160°; well-done, 170°). Let stand for 15 minutes before slicing.

YIELD: 25-30 servings.

HOME-STYLE ROAST BEEF

SANDRA FURMAN-KRAJEWSKI, AMSTERDAM, NEW YORK

PREP: 10 min. **BAKE:** 2 ½ hours + standing

1 beef bottom round roast
 (10 to 12 pounds)
1 can (14 ½ ounces) chicken broth
1 can (10 ¼ ounces) beef gravy
1 can (10 ¾ ounces) condensed cream
 of celery soup, undiluted
¼ cup water
¼ cup Worcestershire sauce
¼ cup soy sauce
3 tablespoons dried parsley flakes
3 tablespoons dill weed
2 tablespoons dried thyme
4½ teaspoons garlic powder

QUICK BEEF STEW

VALERIE COOK, HUBBARD, IOWA

PREP/TOTAL TIME: 15 min.

1 can (15 ounces) mixed vegetables
2 cups leftover diced cooked roast beef
1 can (10 ¾ ounces) condensed cream
 of celery soup, undiluted
1 can (10 ¾ ounces) condensed cream
 of mushroom soup, undiluted
½ teaspoon dried thyme, optional
¼ teaspoon dried rosemary, optional
 Pepper to taste

Drain mixed vegetables, reserving liquid. In a saucepan, combine the beef, vegetables, soups and seasonings. Heat through. If desired, add the reserved vegetable liquid to thin the stew.

YIELD: 4 servings.

SPINACH BEEF BAKE

LAVERNE SCHULTZ, GREENFIELD, WISCONSIN

PREP: 10 min. **BAKE:** 45 min.

1	pound ground beef
1	jar (4 1/2 ounces) sliced mushrooms, drained
1	medium onion, chopped
2	garlic cloves, minced
1 1/2	teaspoons dried oregano
1 1/4	teaspoons salt
1/4	teaspoon pepper
2	packages (10 ounces *each*) frozen chopped spinach, thawed and squeezed dry
1	can (10 3/4 ounces) condensed cream of celery soup, undiluted
1	cup (8 ounces) sour cream
1	cup uncooked long grain rice
1	cup (4 ounces) shredded part-skim mozzarella cheese

In a skillet, cook beef over medium heat until no longer pink; drain. Add the mushrooms, onion, garlic, oregano, salt and pepper. Add the spinach, soup, sour cream and rice; mix well.

Transfer to a greased 2 1/2-qt. baking dish. Sprinkle with mozzarella cheese. Cover and bake at 350° for 45-50 minutes or until the rice is tender.

YIELD: 6-8 servings.

TORTILLA BEEF BAKE

KIM OSBURN, LIGONIER, INDIANA

PREP: 10 min. **BAKE:** 30 min.

1 1/2	pounds ground beef
1	can (10 3/4 ounces) condensed cream of chicken soup, undiluted
2 1/2	cups crushed tortilla chips, *divided*
1	jar (16 ounces) salsa
1 1/2	cups (6 ounces) shredded cheddar cheese

In a skillet, cook beef over medium heat until no longer pink; drain. Stir in soup. Sprinkle 1 1/2 cups tortilla chips in a greased shallow 2 1/2-qt. baking dish. Top with beef mixture, salsa and cheese.

Bake, uncovered, at 350° for 25-30 minutes or until bubbly. Sprinkle with the remaining chips. Bake 3 minutes longer or until chips are lightly toasted.

YIELD: 6 servings.

MARZETTI

MARGARET ADAMS, NORTH VERNON, INDIANA

PREP: 15 min. **BAKE:** 45 min.

1	pound ground beef
1	large onion, chopped
$1/2$	green pepper, chopped
1	can (10 $3/4$ ounces) condensed cream of mushroom soup, undiluted
1	can (10 $3/4$ ounces) condensed tomato soup, undiluted
1	can (6 ounces) tomato paste
1	teaspoon salt
$1/4$	teaspoon dried oregano
$1/4$	teaspoon pepper
$1/3$	cup water
1	tablespoon Worcestershire sauce
8	ounces wide noodles, cooked and drained
1	cup (4 ounces) shredded cheddar cheese

In a large skillet, cook the beef, onion and green pepper over medium heat until meat is no longer pink and vegetables are tender; drain. Stir in the soups, tomato paste, seasonings, water, Worcestershire sauce and noodles.

Spoon into a greased shallow 3-qt. baking dish; top with cheese. Cover and bake at 350° for 45 minutes or until heated through.

YIELD: 4-6 servings.

BEEF-STUFFED SOPAIPILLAS

LARA PENNELL, IRVING, TEXAS

PREP/TOTAL TIME: 30 min.

2	cups all-purpose flour
1	teaspoon salt
1	teaspoon baking powder
1/2	cup water
1/4	cup evaporated milk
1 1/2	teaspoons vegetable oil
	Additional oil for frying

FILLING:

1	pound ground beef
3/4	cup chopped onion
1/2	teaspoon salt
1/2	teaspoon garlic powder
1/4	teaspoon pepper

SAUCE:

1	can (10 3/4 ounces) condensed cream of chicken soup, undiluted
1/2	cup chicken broth
1	can (4 ounces) chopped green chilies
1/2	teaspoon onion powder
2	cups (8 ounces) shredded cheddar cheese

In a bowl, combine the flour, salt and baking powder. Stir in the water, milk and oil with a fork until a ball forms. On a lightly floured surface, knead dough gently for 2-3 minutes. Cover and let stand for 15 minutes. Divide into four portions; roll each into a 6 1/2-in. circle.

In an electric skillet or deep-fat fryer, heat oil to 375°. Fry circles, one at a time, for 2-3 minutes on each side or until golden brown. Drain on paper towels.

In a skillet, cook beef and onion over medium heat until meat is no longer pink; drain. Stir in the salt, garlic powder and pepper. In a saucepan, combine the soup, broth, chilies and onion powder; cook for 10 minutes or until heated through. Cut a slit on one side of each sopaipilla; fill with 1/2 cup of meat mixture. Top with cheese. Serve with sauce.

YIELD: 4 servings.

BEEF AND POTATO CASSEROLE

BRENDA BRADSHAW, OCONTO, WISCONSIN

PREP: 15 min. **BAKE:** 25 min.

4	cups frozen potato rounds
1	pound ground beef
1	package (10 ounces) frozen chopped broccoli, thawed
1	can (10 3/4 ounces) condensed cream of celery soup, undiluted
1/3	cup milk
1	cup (4 ounces) shredded cheddar cheese, *divided*
1/4	teaspoon garlic powder
1/8	teaspoon pepper

Place potato rounds on the bottom and up the sides of a 13-in. x 9-in. x 2-in. baking dish. Bake at 400° for 10 minutes.

Meanwhile, cook beef over medium heat until no longer pink; drain. Place beef and broccoli over potatoes. Combine the soup, milk, 1/2 cup cheddar cheese, garlic powder and pepper. Pour over beef mixture.

Cover and bake at 400° for 20 minutes. Uncover; spinkle with remaining cheese. Bake 2 to 3 minutes longer or until the cheese is melted.

YIELD: 6 servings.

Combine salsa and soup; pour down the center of enchiladas. Sprinkle with remaining cheese. Bake one casserole, uncovered, at 350° for 20-25 minutes or until heated through and cheese is melted. Cover and freeze remaining casserole for up to 3 months.

YIELD: 2 casseroles (5-6 enchiladas each).

TO USE FROZEN CASSEROLE: Thaw in the refrigerator overnight. Cover and bake at 350° for 30 minutes. Uncover; bake 5-10 minutes longer or until heated through and cheese is melted.

CHEDDAR BEEF ENCHILADAS

STACY CIZEK, CONRAD, IOWA

PREP: 30 min. BAKE: 20 min.

- 1 pound ground beef
- 1 envelope taco seasoning
- 1 cup water
- 2 cups cooked rice
- 1 can (16 ounces) refried beans
- 2 cups (8 ounces) shredded cheddar cheese, *divided*
- 10 to 12 flour tortillas (8 inches)
- 1 jar (16 ounces) salsa
- 1 can (10 3/4 ounces) condensed cream of chicken soup, undiluted

In a large skillet, cook beef over medium heat until no longer pink; drain. Stir in taco seasoning and water. Bring to a boil. Reduce heat; simmer, uncovered, for 5 minutes. Stir in rice. Cook and stir until liquid is evaporated.

Spread about 2 tablespoons of refried beans, 1/4 cup beef mixture and 1 tablespoon cheese down the center of each tortilla; roll up. Place seam side down in two greased 13-in. x 9-in. x 2-in. baking dishes.

BEEFY RANCH BEANS

SUE NEELD, DUNCAN, OKLAHOMA

PREP/TOTAL TIME: 30 min.

- 2 pounds ground beef
- 1 medium onion, chopped
- 2 cans (15 ounces *each*) ranch-style beans or chili beans
- 2 cans (10 3/4 ounces *each*) condensed cream of chicken soup, undiluted
- 2 cans (10 ounces *each*) diced tomatoes and green chilies
- 1 jar (8 ounces) taco sauce

In a soup kettle or Dutch oven, cook beef and onion over medium heat until the meat is no longer pink; drain. Add the remaining ingredients. Cook, uncovered, over medium heat until heated through, about 10 minutes.

YIELD: 8-10 servings.

Broccoli Beef Supper

CONNIE BOLTON, SAN ANTONIO, TEXAS

PREP: 15 min. **BAKE:** 35 min.

4	cups frozen cottage fries
1	pound ground beef
1	package (10 ounces) frozen chopped broccoli, thawed
1	can (2.8 ounces) french-fried onions, *divided*
1	medium tomato, chopped
1	can (10 ¾ ounces) condensed cream of celery soup, undiluted
1	cup (4 ounces) shredded cheddar cheese, *divided*
½	cup milk
¼	teaspoon garlic powder
¼	teaspoon pepper

Line bottom and sides of a greased 13-in. x 9-in. x 2-in. baking dish with cottage fries. Bake, uncovered, at 400° for 10 minutes.

Meanwhile, in a skillet, cook beef over medium heat until no longer pink; drain. Layer the beef, broccoli, half of the onions and the tomato over fries. In a bowl, combine the soup, ½ cup cheese, milk, garlic powder and pepper; pour over top.

Cover and bake at 400° for 20 minutes. Uncover; sprinkle with remaining cheese and onions. Bake 2 minutes longer or until cheese is melted.

YIELD: 8 servings.

Vegetable Beef Pie

VALORIE HALL WALKER, BRADLEY, SOUTH CAROLINA

PREP: 15 min. **BAKE:** 30 min.

	Pastry for double-crust pie (9 inches)
1	pound ground beef, cooked and drained
1	can (15 ounces) mixed vegetables, drained *or* 1 ½ cups frozen mixed vegetables
1	can (10 ¾ ounces) condensed cream of onion soup, undiluted
½	teaspoon pepper

Line a 9-in. pie plate with bottom pastry. In a bowl, combine the beef, vegetables, soup and pepper. Spoon into crust. Roll out the remaining pastry to fit top of pie. Place over filling; trim, seal and flute edges. Cut slits in top. Bake at 400° for 30-35 minutes or until crust is golden brown.

YIELD: 4-6 servings.

Meatball Stroganoff with Noodles

CAROL SCHURVINSKE, GENESEO, ILLINOIS

PREP: 40 min. + standing COOK: 15 min.

- 2 cups all-purpose flour
- 1 teaspoon salt
- 3 egg yolks
- 1 egg
- 6 tablespoons water

MEATBALLS:

- 1 egg, lightly beaten
- 2 tablespoons ketchup
- 1/4 cup quick-cooking oats
- 1 tablespoon finely chopped onion
- 1/2 teaspoon salt
- 1 pound ground beef

SAUCE:

- 2 cans (10 3/4 ounces *each*) condensed cream of mushroom soup, undiluted
- 1 cup (8 ounces) sour cream
- 1 cup milk
- 1 tablespoon paprika
- 2 quarts water
- 1 teaspoon salt
- 1 tablespoon butter
- 1 tablespoon minced parsley

In a bowl, combine the flour and salt; make a well. Beat yolks, egg and water; pour into well and stir. Turn onto a floured surface; knead 8-10 times. Divide into thirds; roll out each as thin as possible. Let stand for 20 minutes or until partially dried. Cut into 1/4-in. strips, then into 2-in. pieces; set aside.

In a bowl, combine the egg, ketchup, oats, onion and salt. Crumble beef over mixture and mix well. Shape into 1 1/2-in. balls. Place in a greased 11-in. x 7-in. x 2-in. baking dish. Bake, uncovered, at 400° for 10-15 minutes or until no longer pink.

In a large saucepan, combine the soup, sour cream, milk and paprika; heat through. Add meatballs; cover and cook until heated through, stirring frequently.

In another saucepan, bring water and salt to a boil; add noodles. Cook for 12-15 minutes or until tender; drain. Toss with butter and parsley. Serve with meatballs.

YIELD: 6 servings.

Creamy Beef Casserole

MELANIE RILEY, MCHENRY, ILLINOIS

PREP: 20 min. BAKE: 30 min.

- 6 ounces medium egg noodles
- 2 pounds ground beef
- 1 large onion, chopped
- 1 can (15 1/4 ounces) whole kernel corn, drained
- 1 can (10 3/4 ounces) condensed cream of chicken soup, undiluted
- 1 can (10 3/4 ounces) condensed cream of mushroom soup, undiluted
- 1 cup (8 ounces) sour cream
- 1 can (2 ounces) diced pimientos, drained
- 3/4 teaspoon salt
- 1/4 teaspoon pepper
- 1 cup soft bread crumbs
- 1/4 cup butter, melted

Cook noodles according to package directions. Meanwhile, in a skillet, cook beef and onion over medium heat until meat is no longer pink; drain. Drain noodles and add to skillet along with the corn, soups, sour cream, pimientos, salt and pepper; mix well.

Transfer to a greased 3-qt. baking dish. Toss bread crumbs and butter; sprinkle over casserole. Bake, uncovered, at 350° for 30 minutes or until heated through.

YIELD: 8 servings.

PASA DE SHUTO

MARTY MARTIN, OGDEN, UTAH

PREP/TOTAL TIME: 20 min.

- 1   pound bulk sausage
- 1   pound ground beef
- 6   cups chopped mixed vegetables (carrots, onions, green peppers, fresh mushrooms and celery)
- 1   can (10 3/4 ounces) condensed tomato soup, undiluted
- 1   can (10 3/4 ounces) condensed cream of mushroom soup, undiluted
- 1   can (8 ounces) tomato sauce
- 2   teaspoons chili powder
- 1/2   teaspoon ground cloves
- 1/2   teaspoon ground cinnamon
- 1/2   teaspoon salt
- 1   package (12 ounces) thin spaghetti, broken into 1-inch lengths

In a large skillet, cook sausage and beef over medium heat until no longer pink; drain. Add vegetables and saute just until crisp-tender.

Stir in the soups, tomato sauce and seasonings. Meanwhile, cook spaghetti according to package directions; drain. Add to skillet and stir gently to mix.

YIELD: 10-12 servings.

PORK

CHEESY BRATWURST (pictured left)

KIM MIERS, ROCK ISLAND, ILLINOIS

PREP: 20 min. **COOK:** 20 min.

4	medium potatoes, peeled and cut into $1/2$-inch cubes
2	cups water, *divided*
6	fully cooked bratwurst links (1 pound), cut into $1/2$-inch slices
1	can (10 $3/4$ ounces) condensed cream of mushroom soup, undiluted
2	cups frozen cut green beans
1	small onion, chopped
1	cup (4 ounces) shredded cheddar cheese

Place potatoes and 1 cup water in a deep skillet or large saucepan; bring to a boil. Reduce heat; cook for 15 minutes or until almost tender. Drain and set aside.

In the same pan, brown bratwurst. Add the soup, beans, onion, potatoes and remaining water. Cover and simmer for 15 minutes or until the vegetables are tender. Add cheese, stirring until cheese is melted.

YIELD: 6 servings.

COUNTRY PORK CHOP DINNER

JEAN LAWSON, DOVER, DELAWARE

PREP: 15 min. **COOK:** 25 min.

4	pork loin chops ($1/2$ inch thick)
1	small onion, chopped
1	tablespoon canola oil
4	medium red potatoes, cubed
1	cup halved baby carrots *or* thinly sliced carrots
1	jar (4 $1/2$ ounces) sliced mushrooms *or* 1 cup sliced fresh mushrooms
1	can (10 $3/4$ ounces) condensed cream of celery soup, undiluted
$1/2$	cup water
1	teaspoon salt, optional
$1/2$	to 1 teaspoon dried thyme

In a large skillet, cook pork and onion in oil until meat is browned; drain. Top with the potatoes, carrots and mushrooms.

Combine the soup, water, salt if desired and thyme; pour over vegetables. Bring to a boil; reduce heat. Cover and simmer for 25-30 minutes or until vegetables are tender.

YIELD: 4 servings.

PORK AND VEGGIE SKILLET

SHERRY SCHONEMAN, CEDAR FALLS, IOWA

PREP: 15 min. **BAKE:** 30 min. + standing

6	bone-in pork loin chops (1/2 inch thick)
2	tablespoons vegetable oil
1	teaspoon salt
2	cups water
1	package (10 ounces) frozen French-style green beans
1	cup thinly sliced carrots
1	package (5 ounces) scalloped potatoes
1	can (10 3/4 ounces) condensed cream of celery soup, undiluted
2/3	cup milk
2	tablespoons butter
1/2	teaspoon Worcestershire sauce

In a large skillet, brown pork chops in oil; sprinkle with salt. In a large saucepan, bring the water to a boil; add beans, carrots, potatoes with contents of sauce packet, soup, milk, butter and Worcestershire sauce. Bring to a boil.

Transfer to a greased 13-in. x 9-in. x 2-in. baking dish; top with pork chops. Cover and bake at 350° for 25 minutes. Uncover; bake 5 minutes longer or until pork and vegetables are tender. Let stand for 10 minutes before serving.

YIELD: 6 servings.

DILLED HAM ON RICE

DEBBY COLE, WOLF CREEK, OREGON

PREP/TOTAL TIME: 30 min.

4	cups julienned fully cooked ham
2	tablespoons butter
2	celery ribs, thinly sliced
1	medium onion, chopped
1	cup sliced fresh mushrooms
1	can (10 3/4 ounces) condensed cream of chicken soup, undiluted
1/4	to 1/2 cup milk
2	teaspoons prepared mustard
1/4	to 1/2 teaspoon dill weed
1/2	cup sour cream
	Hot cooked rice

In a large skillet, cook ham in butter until lightly browned. Add the celery, onion and mushrooms; saute until tender. Combine the soup, milk, mustard and dill; add to the ham mixture. Bring to a boil; reduce heat. Stir in sour cream; heat through. Serve over rice.

YIELD: 6 servings.

BACON TATER BAKE

NITA CINQUINA, SURPRISE, ARIZONA

PREP: 10 min. **BAKE:** 1 hour

2	cans (10 3/4 ounces *each*) condensed cream of mushroom soup, undiluted
1 1/3	cups sour cream
1	large onion, chopped
1	pound sliced bacon, cooked and crumbled
1	package (32 ounces) frozen Tater Tots

In a large bowl, combine the soup, sour cream and onion. Add the bacon and Tater Tots; stir until combined. Transfer to a greased 13-in. x 9-in. x 2-in. baking dish. Cover and bake at 350° for 50 minutes. Uncover; bake 8-10 minutes longer or until golden brown.

YIELD: 10 servings.

CHICKEN-BAKED CHOPS

DEBBIE SMITH, BROKEN ARROW, OKLAHOMA

PREP: 10 min. **BAKE:** 1 hour

4	bone-in pork chops (1/2 inch thick)
1	tablespoon vegetable oil
1	can (10 3/4 ounces) condensed cream of chicken soup, undiluted
1/2	cup water
3	tablespoons Worcestershire sauce
1/4	teaspoon salt
1/8	teaspoon pepper

In a large skillet, brown the pork chops in oil. Transfer to a greased 13-in. x 9-in. x 2-in. baking dish. Combine the remaining ingredients; pour over chops. Cover and bake at 350° for 1 hour or until meat juices run clear.

YIELD: 4 servings.

COOKING TIP

The thickness of pork chops affects the cooking time. For thinner chops, reduce the cooking time. For thicker pork chops, check doneness at minimum time and if necessary, cook a little longer.

SAUSAGE SKILLET SUPPER

CATHY WILLIAMS, AURORA, MINNESOTA

PREP/TOTAL TIME: 30 min.

- 1 pound smoked sausage links, cut into ½-inch slices
- ¾ cup uncooked instant rice
- 1 can (10 ¾ ounces) condensed cream of celery soup, undiluted
- ¾ cup water
- 1 tablespoon butter
- 1 package (10 ounces) frozen peas
- 1 can (4 ounces) mushroom stems and pieces, drained
- 1 cup (4 ounces) shredded Swiss cheese

In a large skillet, combine the sausage, rice, soup, water and butter. Bring to a boil. Reduce heat; cover and simmer for 5 minutes. Stir in peas and mushrooms. Cover and simmer for 20 minutes or until rice is tender. Sprinkle with cheese.

YIELD: 4 servings.

PORK NOODLE CASSEROLE

BERNICE MORRIS, MARSHFIELD, MISSOURI

PREP: 15 min. BAKE: 30 min.

- 2 cups uncooked egg noodles
- 2 pounds boneless pork, cut into ¾-inch cubes
- 2 medium onions, chopped
- 2 cans (15 ¼ ounces *each*) whole kernel corn, drained
- 2 cans (10 ¾ ounces *each*) condensed cream of mushroom soup, undiluted
- ½ teaspoon salt
- ½ teaspoon pepper

Cook noodles according to package directions. In a large skillet, cook pork and onions over medium heat until meat is no longer pink. Drain noodles. Stir the noodles, corn, soup, salt and pepper into pork mixture.

Transfer to a greased 3-qt. baking dish. Cover and bake at 350° for 30 minutes. Uncover; bake 15 minutes longer.

YIELD: 8 servings.

COOKING TIP

Sausage Skillet Supper is a quick dish that's ideal for a busy weeknight. You can easily modify it to suit your family's tastes. Simply substitute a package of corn, green beans or broccoli for the peas.

PIZZA RIGATONI

MARILYN COWAN, NORTH MANCHESTER, INDIANA

PREP: 15 min. **COOK:** 4 hours

3	cups uncooked rigatoni *or* large tube pasta
1½	pounds bulk Italian sausage
4	cups (16 ounces) shredded part-skim mozzarella cheese
1	can (10¾ ounces) condensed cream of mushroom soup, undiluted
1	small onion, chopped
2	cans (one 15 ounces, one 8 ounces) pizza sauce
1	package (3½ ounces) sliced pepperoni
1	can (6 ounces) pitted ripe olives, drained and halved

Cook pasta according to package directions. Meanwhile, in a large skillet, cook sausage over medium heat until no longer pink; drain. Drain pasta.

In a 5-qt. slow cooker, layer half of the sausage, pasta, cheese, soup, onion, pizza sauce, pepperoni and olives. Repeat layers. Cover and cook on low for 4 hours.

YIELD: 6-8 servings.

POTATO HAM BAKE

ARTHUR HEIDORN, HILLSIDE, ILLINOIS

PREP: 10 min. **BAKE:** 1 hour 25 min.

3	medium potatoes, peeled and thinly sliced
2	cups cubed fully cooked ham
1	medium onion, sliced and separated into rings
8	slices process American cheese
1	can (10¾ ounces) condensed cream of mushroom soup, undiluted
½	cup frozen peas, thawed

In a greased shallow 3-qt. baking dish, layer with half of the potatoes, ham, onion, cheese and soup. Repeat layers.

Cover and bake at 350° for 1¼ hours or until potatoes are almost tender. Uncover; sprinkle with peas. Bake 10 minutes longer or until heated through.

YIELD: 6 servings.

VEGGIE NOODLE HAM CASSEROLE

JUDY MOODY, WHEATLEY, ONTARIO

PREP: 15 min. **BAKE:** 50 min.

1	package (12 ounces) wide egg noodles
1	can (10 ¾ ounces) condensed cream of chicken soup, undiluted
1	can (10 ¾ ounces) condensed cream of broccoli soup, undiluted
1½	cups milk
2	cups frozen corn, thawed
1½	cups frozen California-blend vegetables, thawed
1½	cups cubed fully cooked ham
2	tablespoons minced fresh parsley
½	teaspoons pepper
¼	teaspoon salt
1	cup (4 ounces) shredded cheddar cheese, *divided*

Cook noodles according to package directions; drain. In a bowl, combine soups and milk; stir in the noodles, corn, vegetables, ham, parsley, pepper, salt and ¾ cup of cheese. Transfer to a greased 13-in. x 9-in. x 2-in. baking dish.

Cover and bake at 350° for 45 minutes. Uncover; sprinkle with remaining cheese. Bake 5-10 minutes longer or until bubbly and cheese is melted.

YIELD: 8-10 servings.

POLISH REUBEN DISH

IMOGENE PETERSON, ONTARIO, OREGON

PREP: 20 min. BAKE: 30 min.

- 1 package (8 ounces) egg noodles
- 2 cans (14 ounces *each*) Bavarian sauerkraut, drained
- 2 cans (10 $^3/_4$ ounces *each*) condensed cream of mushroom soup, undiluted
- 1 $^1/_3$ cups milk
- 1 medium onion, chopped
- 1 tablespoon prepared mustard
- 1 $^1/_2$ pounds smoked kielbasa *or* Polish sausage, halved lengthwise and cut into $^1/_2$-inch slices
- 2 cups (8 ounces) shredded Swiss cheese
- $^1/_2$ cup soft rye bread crumbs
- 2 tablespoons butter, melted

Cook noodles according to package directions; drain. Spread sauerkraut in a greased shallow 4-qt. baking dish. Top with noodles. In a bowl, combine the soup, milk, onion and mustard; pour over the noodles. Top with sausage; sprinkle with cheese.

Combine bread crumbs and butter; sprinkle over the top. Cover and bake at 350° for 30-35 minutes or until heated through.

YIELD: 12-14 servings.

COOKING TIP | Any leftover smoked sausage can be wrapped in plastic wrap and placed in a freezer container. It can be frozen for 1 to 2 months.

PORK CHOP SUPPER

KATHY THOMPSON, PORT ORANGE, FLORIDA

PREP: 10 min. COOK: 30 min.

- 4 pork loin chops ($^1/_2$ inch thick)
- 1 tablespoon butter
- 3 medium red potatoes, cut into small wedges
- 2 cups baby carrots *or* 3 medium carrots, sliced $^1/_2$ inch thick
- 1 medium onion, quartered
- 1 can (10 $^3/_4$ ounces) condensed cream of mushroom soup, undiluted
- $^1/_4$ cup water

In a large skillet, brown pork chops in butter over medium heat for 3 minutes on each side. Add the potatoes, carrots and onion. Combine soup and water; pour over the top. Cover and simmer for 15-20 minutes or until the vegetables are tender.

YIELD: 4 servings.

SCALLOPED POTATOES AND PORK CHOPS

SUSAN CHAVEZ, VANCOUVER, WASHINGTON

PREP: 10 min. **BAKE:** 1¼ hours

5	cups thinly sliced peeled potatoes
1	cup chopped onion
	Salt and pepper to taste
1	can (10 ¾ ounces) condensed cream of mushroom soup, undiluted
½	cup sour cream
6	pork loin chops (1 inch thick)
	Chopped fresh parsley

In a greased 13-in. x 9-in. x 2-in. baking dish, layer half of the potatoes and onion; sprinkle with salt and pepper. Repeat layers. Combine the soup and sour cream; pour over potato mixture.

Cover and bake at 375° for 30 minutes. Meanwhile in a nonstick skillet, brown pork chops on both sides. Place chops on top of casserole. Cover and bake for 30 minutes. Uncover; bake 15 minutes longer or until chops are tender. Sprinkle with parsley.

YIELD: 6 servings.

HAM NOODLE CASSEROLE

SHERI SWITZER, CRAWFORDVILLE, INDIANA

PREP: 15 min. BAKE: 20 min.

- 6 cups uncooked no-yolk medium noodles
- 1 can (10 3/4 ounces) reduced-fat reduced-sodium condensed cream of celery soup, undiluted
- 1 cup cubed fully cooked lean ham
- 2/3 cup cubed reduced-fat process cheese (Velveeta)
- 1/2 cup fat-free milk
- 1/4 cup thinly sliced green onions
- 1/2 teaspoon curry powder

Cook noodles according to package directions; drain and place in a large bowl. Stir in the remaining ingredients.

Transfer to a shallow 2 1/2-qt. baking dish coated with nonstick cooking spray. Cover and bake at 375° for 20-30 minutes or until heated through.

YIELD: 6 servings.

COUNTRY SUPPER

ARLENE SNYDER, EPHRATA, PENNSYLVANIA

PREP/TOTAL TIME: 15 min.

- 1 small onion, chopped
- 1 tablespoon vegetable oil
- 1 can (10 3/4 ounces) condensed cream of celery soup, undiluted
- 1/2 cup milk
- 1 teaspoon Worcestershire sauce
- 1/4 teaspoon salt
- 1/8 teaspoon pepper
- 1 cup cubed cooked pork

- 1 cup cubed cooked potatoes
- 1 cup frozen peas, thawed
  Biscuits, optional

In a large skillet, saute onion in oil until tender. Stir in the soup, milk, Worcestershire, salt and pepper; mix well. Add the pork, potatoes and peas; heat through. Serve with biscuits if desired.

YIELD: 2-3 servings.

SAUSAGE STROGANOFF

TERESA NIESEN, RAPID CITY, SOUTH DAKOTA

PREP/TOTAL TIME: 30 min.

- 1 package (12 ounces) medium egg noodles
- 1 pound fully cooked smoked sausage, cut into 1/2-inch pieces
- 1 can (10 3/4 ounces) condensed cream of chicken soup, undiluted
- 1 cup (8 ounces) sour cream
- 2 tablespoons grated Parmesan cheese
- 1/4 teaspoon seasoned salt
- 1/8 teaspoon pepper
- 2 tablespoons butter

Cook noodles according to package directions. Meanwhile, in a large skillet, cook sausage over medium heat until heated through; drain. Remove with a slotted spoon and keep warm.

Combine the soup, sour cream, Parmesan cheese, seasoned salt and pepper; set aside. Melt butter in the skillet. Drain noodles and add to skillet. Add soup mixture and sausage; toss to coat. Heat through.

YIELD: 6 servings.

PORK CHOPS AND FRIES

ANITA BAFIK, AVONMORE, PENNSYLVANIA

PREP: 15 min. **BAKE:** 25 min.

- 1/2 teaspoon salt
- 1/8 teaspoon pepper
- 1/8 teaspoon paprika
- 4 bone-in pork loin chops (1/2 inch thick)
- 2 tablespoons vegetable oil
- 1 can (10 3/4 ounces) condensed cream of mushroom soup, undiluted
- 1/2 cup sour cream
- 2 tablespoons milk
- 1 teaspoon dried parsley flakes
- 4 cups frozen steaks fries, thawed
- 2 cups frozen cut green beans, thawed

Combine the salt, pepper and paprika; sprinkle over pork chops. In a large skillet, brown chops in oil on each side; drain. Remove chops and keep warm. In the same skillet, combine the soup, sour cream, milk and parsley; cook and stir until heated through.

In a greased 11-in. x 7-in. x 2-in. baking dish, layer fries, beans and soup mixture. Top with chops. Cover and bake at 350° for 20 minutes. Uncover; bake 5-10 minutes longer or until meat is tender and vegetables are heated through.

YIELD: 4 servings.

BROCCOLI HAM DIVAN

MRS. L.M. RENFROW, SHAWNEE MISSION, KANSAS

PREP/TOTAL TIME: 30 min.

- 1 can (10 3/4 ounces) condensed cream of mushroom soup, undiluted
- 1/4 cup milk
- 1 teaspoon prepared mustard
- 1/2 teaspoon Worcestershire sauce
- Dash pepper
- 2 packages (10 ounces *each*) frozen broccoli pieces, cooked and drained
- 2 cups cubed fully cooked ham
- 1 can (6 ounces) french-fried onions, *divided*
- 1 cup (4 ounces) shredded cheddar cheese

Combine the soup, milk, mustard, Worcestershire sauce and pepper; spoon half into a skillet. Top with the broccoli, ham, half of the onions and cheese. Spoon remaining soup mixture over cheese and top with remaining onions.

Cover and cook over low heat for 20-25 minutes or until heated through. Do not stir.

YIELD: 4-6 servings.

HOT SAUSAGE AND RICE

DELENE DURHAM, CAMPBELLSVILLE, KENTUCKY

PREP: 10 min. **BAKE:** 30 min.

- 1 pound bulk hot pork sausage
- 1 medium onion, chopped
- 3 cups cooked rice
- 1 *each* medium green, sweet red and yellow peppers, diced
- 1 can (10 3/4 ounces) condensed cream of mushroom soup, undiluted
- 1 can (10 1/2 ounces) condensed French onion soup, undiluted

In a large skillet over medium heat, cook sausage and onion until the sausage is browned and onion is tender; drain. Add the rice, peppers and soups; mix well.

Transfer to an ungreased 13-in. x 9-in. x 2-in. baking dish. Bake, uncovered, at 350° for 30-35 minutes or until bubbly.

YIELD: 6-8 servings.

Ham 'n' Chicken Noodle Bake

CONNIE SANDEN, MENTOR, OHIO

PREP: 25 min. **BAKE:** 45 min.

1	cup chopped onion
2	tablespoons butter
2	cups cubed fully cooked ham
2	cups diced cooked chicken
1	medium green pepper, chopped
1/2	cup chopped sweet red pepper
1	cup whole pimento-stuffed green olives
1	can (10 3/4 ounces) condensed cream of mushroom soup, undiluted
1	cup (8 ounces) sour cream
1 1/2	teaspoons salt
1/4	teaspoon pepper
8	ounces noodles, cooked and drained
3	tablespoons shredded Parmesan cheese

In a skillet, saute onion in butter until tender. In a large bowl, combine the ham, chicken, peppers, olives, soup, sour cream, salt, pepper and onion. Fold in noodles.

Pour into a greased shallow 2 1/2-qt. baking dish. Sprinkle with the Parmesan cheese. Bake, uncovered, at 325° for 45 minutes or until bubbly.

YIELD: 8 servings.

HASH BROWN PORK BAKE

DARLIS WILFER, PHELPS, WISCONSIN

PREP: 15 min. **BAKE:** 1 hour

2	cups (16 ounces) sour cream
1	can (10 3/4 ounces) condensed cream of chicken soup, undiluted
1	package (32 ounces) frozen cubed hash brown potatoes, thawed
2	cups cubed cooked pork
1	pound process cheese (Velveeta), cubed
1/4	cup chopped onion
2	cups crushed cornflakes
1/2	cup butter, melted
1	cup (4 ounces) shredded part-skim mozzarella cheese
3	green pepper rings

In a large bowl, combine sour cream and soup. Stir in the hash browns, pork, process cheese and onion.

Transfer to a greased shallow 3-qt. baking dish. Toss cornflake crumbs and butter; sprinkle over the top. Bake, uncovered, at 350° for 50 minutes. Sprinkle with mozzarella cheese. Bake 10 minutes longer or until bubbly. Garnish with green pepper rings.

YIELD: 8 servings.

VEGGIES AND HAM

BARB SEARS, FALCONER, NEW YORK

PREP/TOTAL TIME: 30 min.

3	cups frozen cut green beans, thawed
2	cups frozen corn, thawed
2	tablespoons butter
1	tablespoon all-purpose flour
1	can (10 3/4 ounces) condensed cream of chicken soup, undiluted
1/2	cup sour cream
2	cups cubed cooked ham
1	cup (4 ounces) shredded cheddar cheese

In a large skillet, saute the green beans and corn in butter. Sprinkle with flour; mix well.

In a bowl, combine the soup, sour cream and ham. Stir into vegetable mixture. Cook over medium heat until heated through. Remove from the heat. Sprinkle with the cheese; cover and let stand for 3 minutes or until cheese is melted.

YIELD: 4 servings.

CROWD-SIZE SAUSAGE 'N' NOODLES

JULIA LIVINGSTON, FROSTPROOF, FLORIDA

PREP: 20 min. BAKE: 30 min.

- 1   package (16 ounces) egg noodles
- 2   pounds bulk pork sausage
- 2   cans (10 3/4 ounces *each*) condensed cream of chicken soup, undiluted
- 2   cups (16 ounces) sour cream
- 1   cup crumbled blue cheese
- 2   jars (4 1/2 ounces *each*) sliced mushrooms, drained
- 1   jar (4 ounces) diced pimientos, drained
- 1/4 cup finely chopped green pepper
- 1   cup soft bread crumbs
- 2   tablespoons butter, melted

Cook noodles according to package directions. Meanwhile, in a large skillet, cook sausage over medium heat until no longer pink; drain. Drain noodles.

In a Dutch oven, combine the soup, sour cream and blue cheese; cook and stir over medium heat until cheese is melted. Stir in the noodles, sausage, mushrooms, pimientos and green pepper.

Transfer to two greased shallow 3-qt. baking dishes. Toss bread crumbs and butter; sprinkle over top. Bake, uncovered, at 350° for 30-35 minutes or until edges are bubbly.

YIELD: 2 casseroles (8 servings each).

COOKING TIP

To make just one Sausage 'n' Noodles casserole, divide the ingredients in half. For the jar of pimientos, use 2 tablespoons of diced pimientos.

STOVETOP PORK DINNER

CONNIE MOORE, MEDWAY, OHIO

PREP: 10 min. COOK: 50 min.

- 4   bone-in pork loin chops (1/2 inch thick)
- 8   small new potatoes, optional
- 1   small onion, chopped
- 1   can (10 3/4 ounces) condensed cream of chicken soup, undiluted
- 1   can (4 ounces) sliced mushrooms, drained
- 1/4 cup water
- 1/2 teaspoon garlic salt
- 1/2 teaspoon Worcestershire sauce
- 1/4 teaspoon dried thyme
- 1   package (10 ounces) frozen peas and carrots

In a large skillet, brown chops on each side; drain. Add potatoes if desired and onion. Combine the soup, mushrooms, water, garlic salt, Worcestershire sauce and thyme; pour into skillet. Bring to a boil. Reduce heat; cover and simmer for 40-45 minutes.

Stir in peas and carrots; cover and simmer for 10 minutes or until heated through.

YIELD: 4 servings.

In a large skillet, brown pork in oil over medium heat for 5 minutes on each side. Transfer to a 13-in. x 9-in. x 2-in. baking dish; keep warm. In the same skillet, saute mushrooms in butter until tender. Stir in the soup, sour cream and broth; pour over pork.

Cover and bake at 325° for 40-50 minutes or until pork is tender.

YIELD: 6-8 servings.

NO-FUSS HAM BAKE

ELAINE GREEN, MECHANICSVILLE, MARYLAND

PREP: 10 min. **BAKE:** 30 min.

1 1/2	pounds fully cooked ham, cubed
1	package (16 ounces) frozen cut broccoli, thawed and drained
2 1/2	cups milk, *divided*
1	can (10 3/4 ounces) condensed cream of mushroom soup, undiluted
1	can (10 3/4 ounces) condensed cheddar cheese soup, undiluted
1/2	teaspoon onion powder
1/4	teaspoon garlic powder
2	cups biscuit/baking mix
	Minced fresh parsley, optional

In a large bowl, combine the ham, broccoli, 1 cup milk, soups, onion powder and garlic powder. Spoon into an ungreased 13-in. x 9-in. x 2-in. baking dish. Combine biscuit mix and remaining milk. Pour over ham mixture.

Bake, uncovered, at 450° for 30 minutes or until hot and bubbly. Garnish with parsley if desired.

YIELD: 8-10 servings.

CREAMY PORK TENDERLOIN

JANICE CHRISTOFFERSON, EAGLE RIVER, WISCONSIN

PREP: 30 min. **BAKE:** 40 min.

2	pork tenderloins (about 1 pound *each*)
1	egg
1	tablespoon water
1/2	teaspoon dried rosemary, crushed
1/4	teaspoon pepper
	Dash garlic powder
1	cup seasoned bread crumbs
3	tablespoons vegetable oil
1/2	pound fresh mushrooms, sliced
2	tablespoons butter
1	can (10 3/4 ounces) condensed cream of chicken soup, undiluted
1	cup (8 ounces) sour cream
1/4	cup chicken broth

Cut each tenderloin into eight pieces. Flatten each piece to 3/4-in. thickness. In a shallow dish, combine the egg, water and seasonings. Place bread crumbs in another shallow dish. Dip pork into egg mixture, then coat with bread crumbs.

PORK AND GREEN CHILI CASSEROLE

DIANNE ESPOSITE, NEW MIDDLETOWN, OHIO

PREP: 20 min. **BAKE:** 30 min.

1½	pounds boneless pork, cut into ½-inch cubes
1	tablespoon vegetable oil
1	can (15 ounces) black beans, rinsed and drained
1	can (10 ¾ ounces) condensed cream of chicken soup, undiluted
1	can (14 ½ ounces) diced tomatoes, undrained
2	cans (4 ounces *each*) chopped green chilies
1	cup quick-cooking brown rice
¼	cup water
2	to 3 tablespoons salsa
1	teaspoon ground cumin
½	cup shredded cheddar cheese

In a large skillet, saute pork in oil until no longer pink; drain. Add the beans, soup, tomatoes, chilies, rice, water, salsa and cumin; cook and stir until bubbly.

Pour into an ungreased shallow 2-qt. baking dish. Bake, uncovered, at 350° for 30 minutes or until bubbly. Sprinkle with cheese; let stand for 3-5 minutes before serving.

YIELD: 6 servings.

SAUSAGE AND MUSHROOM STEW

ANN NACE, PERKASIE, PENNSYLVANIA

PREP: 10 min. **BAKE:** 1 ¾ hours

2	cans (10 ¾ ounces *each*) condensed cream of mushroom soup, undiluted
1½	pounds smoked kielbasa *or* Polish sausage, cut into 1-inch slices
5	medium potatoes, peeled and cut into 1-inch chunks
4	carrots, peeled and cut into 1-inch pieces
3	medium onions, coarsely chopped
1	cup fresh green beans, halved
¾	pound fresh mushrooms, halved
½	medium head cabbage, coarsely chopped

In an ovenproof 5-qt. Dutch oven or baking dish, combine the first seven ingredients. Cover and bake at 350° for 1¼ hours.

Uncover and stir. Add the cabbage. Cover and bake 30 minutes longer or until vegetables are tender. Stir again before serving.

YIELD: 6-8 servings.

HOME-STYLE COOKING WITH CREAM SOUP | **PORK**

Pork Chop Potato Casserole

NORMA SHEPLER, LAKE WALES, FLORIDA

PREP: 10 min. **BAKE:** 45 min.

8	pork chops (1/2 inch thick)
1	teaspoon seasoned salt
1	tablespoon vegetable oil
1	can (10 3/4 ounces) condensed cream of celery soup, undiluted
2/3	cup milk
1/2	cup sour cream
1/2	teaspoon salt
1/4	teaspoon pepper
1	package (26 ounces) frozen shredded hash brown potatoes
1	cup (4 ounces) shredded cheddar cheese, *divided*
1	can (2.8 ounces) french-fried onions, *divided*

Sprinkle pork chops with seasoned salt. In a skillet, brown chops on both sides in oil in batches.

In a large bowl, combine the soup, milk, sour cream, salt and pepper; stir in hash browns, 3/4 cup cheese and half of the onions. Spread into a greased 13-in. x 9-in. x 2-in. baking dish. Arrange pork chops on top.

Cover and bake at 350° for 40 minutes. Uncover; sprinkle with the remaining cheese and onions. Bake 5-10 minutes longer or until potatoes are tender, cheese is melted and meat juices run clear.

YIELD: 8 servings.

Broccoli Ham Roll-Ups

SUSAN SIMMONS, NORWALK, IOWA

PREP: 15 min. **BAKE:** 40 min.

1	package (10 ounces) frozen chopped broccoli
1	can (10 3/4 ounces) condensed cream of mushroom soup, undiluted
1	cup dry bread crumbs
1/4	cup shredded cheddar cheese
1	tablespoon chopped onion
1 1/2	teaspoons diced pimientos
1/8	teaspoon rubbed sage
1/8	teaspoon dried rosemary, crushed
1/8	teaspoon dried thyme
	Dash pepper
12	slices fully cooked ham (1/8 inch thick)

Cook broccoli according to package directions; drain. In a bowl, combine the soup, bread crumbs, cheese, onion, pimientos and seasonings. Add broccoli; mix well. Spoon 1/4 cup onto each ham slice and roll up.

Arrange in an ungreased 13-in. x 9-in. x 2-in. baking dish. Cover and bake at 350° for 40 minutes or until heated through.

YIELD: 12 servings.

PORK HOT DISH

MARIE LEADENS, MAPLE GROVE, MINNESOTA

PREP: 20 min. **BAKE:** 45 min.

1	package (10 ounces) medium egg noodles
1	pound boneless pork, cut into bite-size pieces
1/2	cup chopped celery
1/4	cup chopped sweet red *or* green pepper
1/4	cup chopped onion
1	tablespoon vegetable oil
1	can (10 3/4 ounces) condensed cream of mushroom soup, undiluted
1	can (10 3/4 ounces) condensed cream of chicken soup, undiluted
1	can (14 3/4 ounces) cream-style corn
1/2	cup milk
1	teaspoon salt
1/4	teaspoon pepper
1	cup saltine crumbs
3	tablespoons butter, melted

Cook noodles according to package directions. Meanwhile, in a large skillet, cook the pork, celery, pepper and onion in oil until the meat is browned and vegetables are tender.

Drain noodles. In a large bowl, combine the noodles, pork mixture, soups, corn, milk, salt and pepper.

Transfer to an ungreased 13-in. x 9-in. x 2-in. baking dish. Combine crumbs and butter; sprinkle on top. Bake, uncovered, at 350° for 45 minutes or until heated through.

YIELD: 8-10 servings.

HAM TETRAZZINI

SUSAN BLAIR, STERLING, MICHIGAN

PREP: 15 min. **COOK:** 4 hours

1	can (10 3/4 ounces) reduced-sodium condensed cream of mushroom soup, undiluted
1	cup sliced fresh mushrooms
1	cup cubed fully cooked lean ham
1/2	cup fat-free evaporated milk
2	tablespoons white wine *or* water
1	teaspoon prepared horseradish
1	package (7 ounces) spaghetti
1/2	cup shredded Parmesan cheese

In a 3-qt. slow cooker, combine the soup, mushrooms, ham, milk, wine or water and horseradish. Cover and cook on low for 4 hours.

Cook spaghetti according to package directions; drain. Add the spaghetti and cheese to slow cooker; toss to coat.

YIELD: 6 servings.

OVEN-BAKED CHOP SUEY

NADINE DAHLING, ELKADER, IOWA

PREP: 15 min. **BAKE:** 1 hour

1	package (7 ounces) shell macaroni
2	pounds boneless pork steak, cut into 1-inch pieces
2	cups diced celery
2	medium onions, diced
1	cup chopped green pepper
1	can (10 3/4 ounces) condensed cream of mushroom soup, undiluted
1	can (10 3/4 ounces) condensed cream of chicken soup, undiluted
1	can (4 ounces) mushroom stems and pieces, drained
1/4	cup soy sauce
1	jar (2 ounces) diced pimientos, drained
2	cups chow mein noodles

Cook macaroni according to package directions. Meanwhile, in a large skillet, brown the pork on each side in batches; drain. Drain the macaroni and add to skillet along with the celery, onion, pepper, soups, mushrooms, soy sauce and pimientos; mix well.

Pour into a greased 13-in. x 9-in. x 2-in. baking dish. Top with chow mein noodles. Bake, uncovered, at 350° for 1 to 1 1/4 hours or until heated through.

YIELD: 8 servings.

SPUDS 'N' DOGS

JANET WARE NOVOTNY, GRAND ISLAND, NEBRASKA

PREP: 25 min. **BAKE:** 25 min.

1 1/4	pounds red potatoes, cubed
10	hot dogs (1 pound), sliced
2	tablespoons diced onion
1	cup frozen peas, thawed
1	can (10 3/4 ounces) condensed cream of mushroom soup, undiluted
3	tablespoons butter, melted
1	tablespoon prepared mustard
1/8	teaspoon pepper

Place potatoes in a large saucepan and cover with water. Bring to a boil. Reduce heat; cover and cook for 12-15 minutes or until tender. Drain.

In a greased shallow 2 1/2-qt. baking dish, combine the potatoes, hot dogs, onion and peas. Combine the soup, butter, mustard and pepper; gently stir into potato mixture. Bake, uncovered, at 350° for 25 minutes or until heated through.

YIELD: 6-8 servings.

Ham-It-Up Spaghetti

DONNA GONDA, NORTH CANTON, OHIO

PREP/TOTAL TIME: 30 min.

1	package (16 ounces) spaghetti, broken into 2-inch pieces
2	cans (10 ¾ ounces *each*) condensed cream of mushroom soup, undiluted
1 ¾	cups milk
1	tablespoon dried minced onion
2	teaspoons dried parsley flakes
1	teaspoon Worcestershire sauce
2	cups cubed fully cooked ham (about 1 pound)
2	cups (8 ounces) shredded cheddar cheese

Cook spaghetti according to package directions. Meanwhile, in a large bowl, combine the soup, milk, onion, parsley and Worcestershire sauce. Drain spaghetti; add to soup mixture along with ham.

Transfer to a lightly greased shallow 2½-qt. baking dish. Sprinkle with cheese. Cover and bake at 375° for 15 minutes. Uncover; bake 5 minutes longer or until lightly browned and heated through.

YIELD: 6-8 servings.

Hot Pork Salad Supreme

DAWN EASON, CARMICHAEL, CALIFORNIA

PREP: 10 min. **BAKE:** 30 min.

2	cups diced cooked pork
2	cups cooked rice
1	can (10 ¾ ounces) condensed cream of chicken soup, undiluted
1	cup diced celery
½	cup mayonnaise
1	can (4 ounces) mushroom stems and pieces, drained
1	tablespoon lemon juice
1	tablespoon finely chopped onion
¼	teaspoon salt
1	cup cornflake crumbs
½	cup sliced almonds
2	tablespoons butter, melted

Combine the first nine ingredients; mix well. Spoon into an ungreased 11-in. x 7-in. x 2-in. baking dish.

Combine crumbs, almonds and butter; sprinkle on top. Bake, uncovered, at 350° for 30-40 minutes or until lightly browned.

YIELD: 4-6 servings.

EDITOR'S NOTE: Reduced-fat or fat-free mayonnaise is not recommended for this recipe.

HERB DUMPLINGS WITH PORK CHOPS

CHERYL ONKEN, WILTON, IOWA

PREP: 20 min. **COOK:** 30 min.

- 1 can (10 3/4 ounces) condensed cream of mushroom soup, undiluted
- 1 can (4 ounces) mushroom stems and pieces, undrained
- 1/2 cup water
- 1/2 teaspoon rubbed sage
- 6 bone-in pork loin chops (1/2 inch thick)
- 2 tablespoons vegetable oil
- 1 medium onion, sliced

DUMPLINGS:
- 1 1/2 cups all-purpose flour
- 2 teaspoons baking powder
- 3/4 teaspoon salt
- 1/2 teaspoon celery seed
- 1/2 teaspoon rubbed sage
- 3 tablespoons shortening
- 3/4 cup milk
- 1 tablespoon minced fresh parsley

In a bowl, combine the soup, mushrooms, water and sage; set aside. In a large skillet, brown the pork chops on both sides in oil; top with onion. Pour soup mixture over top. Bring to a boil; reduce heat.

For dumplings, combine the flour, baking powder, salt, celery seed and sage in a bowl. Cut in shortening until mixture resembles coarse crumbs. Stir in milk just until moistened.

Drop by 1/4 cupfuls onto simmering soup mixture; sprinkle with parsley. Simmer, uncovered, for 15 minutes. Cover and simmer 15 minutes longer or until a toothpick inserted in a dumpling comes out clean (do not lift cover while simmering).

YIELD: 6 servings.

BRATS 'N' TOTS

JODI GOBRECHT, BUCYRUS, OHIO

PREP: 20 min. **BAKE:** 35 min.

1	pound uncooked bratwurst, casings removed
1	medium onion, chopped
1	can (10 ¾ ounces) condensed cream of mushroom soup, undiluted
1	package (32 ounces) frozen Tater Tots
2	cups (16 ounces) sour cream
2	cups (8 ounces) shredded cheddar cheese

Crumble bratwurst into a large skillet; add onion. Cook over medium heat until meat is no longer pink; drain. Stir in the soup. Transfer to a greased 13-in. x 9-in. x 2-in. baking dish. Top with Tater Tots and sour cream. Sprinkle with cheese.

Bake, uncovered, at 350° for 35-40 minutes or until heated through and cheese is melted. Let stand for 5 minutes before serving.

YIELD: **6 servings.**

CREAMY POTATOES 'N' KIELBASA

BETH SINE, FAULKNER, MARYLAND

PREP: 5 min. **COOK:** 6 hours

- 1   package (28 ounces) frozen O'Brien hash brown potatoes
- 1   pound smoked kielbasa *or* Polish sausage, cut into 1/4-inch slices
- 1   can (10 3/4 ounces) condensed cream of mushroom soup, undiluted
- 1   cup (4 ounces) shredded cheddar cheese
- 1/2   cup water

In a 3-qt. slow cooker, combine all the ingredients. Cover and cook on low for 6-8 hours or until the potatoes are tender.

YIELD: 4-6 servings.

CARROTS AND CHOPS

MIKE AVERY, BATTLE CREEK, MICHIGAN

PREP: 5 min. **BAKE:** 6 hours

- 6   to 8 medium carrots (1 pound), coarsely chopped
- 3   to 4 medium potatoes, cubed
- 4   boneless pork loin chops (3/4 inch thick)
- 1   large onion, sliced
- 1   envelope onion soup mix
- 2   cans (10 3/4 ounces *each*) condensed cream of mushroom soup, undiluted

Place carrots and potatoes in a 3-qt. slow cooker. Top with the pork chops, onion, soup mix and condensed soup. Cover and cook on low for 6-8 hours or until meat and vegetables are tender.

YIELD: 4 servings.

SPEEDY HAM AND MACARONI

VICKY HARTEL, CALEDONIA, WISCONSIN

PREP/TOTAL TIME: 30 min.

- 2   cups uncooked elbow macaroni
- 1   package (10 ounces) frozen chopped broccoli, thawed
- 1   can (10 3/4 ounces) condensed cream of mushroom soup, undiluted
- 1/2   cup milk
- 1   tablespoon butter
- 1/2   teaspoon ground nutmeg
- 1/8   teaspoon garlic powder
- 1/8   teaspoon pepper
- 2   cups cubed fully cooked ham
      Grated Parmesan cheese, optional

In a large saucepan, cook macaroni in boiling water for 5 minutes. Add broccoli; return to a boil. Cook for 2-3 minutes or until macaroni is tender; drain. Return to the pan.

Combine the soup, milk, butter, nutmeg, garlic powder and pepper; add to macaroni mixture with ham and mix well. Heat through. Garnish with Parmesan cheese if desired.

YIELD: 4-6 servings.

 COOKING TIP | For added convenience, purchase packages of cubed deli ham for recipes like this that call for fully cooked ham.

BAKED RICE WITH SAUSAGE

NAOMI FLOOD, EMPORIA, KANSAS

PREP: 30 min. **BAKE:** 50 min. + standing

2	pounds bulk Italian sausage
4	celery ribs, thinly sliced
1	large onion, chopped
1	large green pepper, chopped
4½	cups water
¾	cup dry chicken noodle soup mix
1	can (10 ¾ ounces) condensed cream of chicken soup, undiluted
1	cup uncooked long grain rice
¼	cup dry bread crumbs
2	tablespoons butter, melted

In a large skillet, cook the sausage, celery, onion and green pepper over medium heat until meat is no longer pink and vegetables are tender; drain. In a large saucepan, bring water to a boil; add dry soup mix. Reduce heat; simmer, uncovered, for 5 minutes or until the noodles are tender. Stir in the condensed soup, rice and sausage mixture; mix well.

Transfer to a greased 13-in. x 9-in. x 2-in. baking dish. Cover and bake at 350° for 40 minutes. Toss bread crumbs with butter. Uncover; sprinkle bread crumbs over rice mixture. Bake 10-15 minutes longer or until rice is tender. Let stand for 10 minutes before serving.

YIELD: 12-14 servings.

PORK POTPIE

DLORES DEWITT, COLORADO SPRINGS, COLORADO

PREP: 20 min. **BAKE:** 20 min.

2	medium carrots, thinly sliced
1	small onion, chopped
¼	cup water
2	cups cubed cooked pork
1	can (10 ¾ ounces) condensed cream of celery soup, undiluted
2	tablespoons minced fresh parsley
¼	teaspoon salt
⅛	teaspoon dried savory
⅛	teaspoon garlic powder
	Pastry for single-crust pie (9 inches)
1	tablespoon grated Parmesan cheese

In a saucepan, bring the carrots, onion and water to a boil. Reduce heat; cover and simmer for 7-9 minutes or until tender. Drain. Add the pork, soup, parsley, salt, savory and garlic powder. Transfer to a greased 9-in. pie plate.

On a lightly floured surface, roll out pastry into 10-in. circle; place over pork mixture. Cut slits in top; flute edges. Sprinkle with Parmesan cheese. Bake at 425° for 18-20 minutes or until golden brown. Let stand for 5 minutes before cutting.

YIELD: 4-6 servings.

ASPARAGUS HAM BAKE

HELEN OSTRONIC, OMAHA, NEBRASKA

PREP: 15 min. **BAKE:** 35 min.

1	pound fresh asparagus, cut into 1-inch pieces
2	cups cubed fully cooked ham
3	cups cooked rice
1	cup diced celery
1½	teaspoons lemon-pepper seasoning
1	can (10 ¾ ounces) condensed cream of chicken soup, undiluted
1	cup chicken broth
1	cup (4 ounces) shredded cheddar cheese
1	tablespoon butter
½	cup bread crumbs

Place asparagus in a large saucepan with enough water to cover. Bring to a boil. Cook, uncovered, for 3-5 minutes or until crisp-tender; drain.

In a large bowl, combine the asparagus, ham, rice, celery and lemon-pepper. Transfer to a greased 2½-qt. baking dish. In a saucepan, combine soup and broth. Add cheese. Cook and stir over medium heat until cheese is melted. Pour over asparagus mixture.

In a small skillet, melt butter; add crumbs and cook and stir until browned. Sprinkle over top of casserole. Bake, uncovered, at 350° for 35 minutes or until heated through.

YIELD: 6-8 servings.

ELEGANT PORK CHOPS

NILA TOWLER, BAIRD, TEXAS

PREP: 10 min. **BAKE:** 50 min. + standing

2	pork loin chops (1 inch thick)
1	tablespoon vegetable oil
1	can (10 ¾ ounces) condensed cream of mushroom soup, undiluted
¾	cup milk
¾	cup uncooked instant rice
⅛	teaspoon onion powder
⅛	teaspoon garlic powder
	Dash pepper

In a skillet, brown the pork chops on each side in oil over medium heat; set aside. In an ungreased 8-in. square baking dish, combine the soup, milk, rice and seasonings. Top with pork chops.

Cover and bake at 350° for 45 minutes or until meat is tender. Uncover; bake 5 minutes longer. Let stand for 10 minutes before serving.

YIELD: 2 servings.

Cook pasta according to package directions; drain. In a greased shallow 3-qt. baking dish, combine the pasta, ham, corn, 1 cup cheese and ¾ cup onions. In a bowl, combine the broth, soup, milk and seasonings. Pour over pasta mixture; mix well.

Bake, uncovered, at 350° for 30 minutes. Sprinkle with remaining cheese and onions. Bake 5 minutes longer or until heated through.

YIELD: 8 servings.

SAUCY PORK CHOPS

SHARON POLK, LAPEER, MICHIGAN

PREP: 5 min. **COOK:** 4 hours

8	boneless pork chops (¹/₂ inch thick)
2	tablespoons vegetable oil
¹/₄	teaspoon salt
¹/₈	teaspoon pepper
2	cans (10 ³/₄ ounces *each*) condensed cream of chicken soup, undiluted
1	medium onion, chopped
¹/₂	cup ketchup
2	tablespoons Worcestershire sauce
	Mashed potatoes *or* hot cooked rice

In a large skillet, cook pork chops in oil until lightly browned on each side. Sprinkle with salt and pepper. Transfer to a 3-qt. slow cooker.

In a bowl, combine the soup, onion, ketchup and Worcestershire sauce; pour over chops. Cover and cook on high for 4-5 hours or until meat juices run clear. Serve over potatoes or rice.

YIELD: 8 servings.

TRICOLOR PASTA WITH HAM

HEATHER ROWAN, THE RICHMOND, MISSOURI

PREP: 15 min. **BAKE:** 35 min.

1	package (16 ounces) tricolor spiral pasta
1¹/₂	cups cubed fully cooked ham
1	can (15 ¹/₄ ounces) whole kernel corn, drained
1¹/₂	cups (6 ounces) shredded cheddar cheese, *divided*
1	can (2.8 ounces) french-fried onions, *divided*
1	can (14 ¹/₂ ounces) chicken broth
1	can (10 ³/₄ ounces) condensed cream of chicken soup, undiluted
¹/₂	cup milk
¹/₂	teaspoon *each* celery salt, garlic powder and pepper

Zucchini Pork Chop Supper

LINDA MARTIN, RHINEBECK, NEW YORK

PREP: 10 min. **BAKE:** 1 hour

- 1 package (14 ounces) seasoned cubed stuffing mix, *divided*
- 1/4 cup butter, melted
- 2 pounds zucchini, cut into 1/2-inch pieces
- 1/2 cup grated carrots
- 1 can (10 3/4 ounces) condensed cream of celery soup, undiluted
- 1/2 cup milk
- 1 cup (8 ounces) sour cream
- 1 tablespoon chopped fresh parsley
- 1/2 teaspoon pepper
- 6 pork loin chops (1 inch thick)
  Water *or* additional milk

Combine two-thirds of the stuffing mix with butter; place half in a greased 13-in. x 9-in. x 2-in. baking dish. Combine the zucchini, carrots, soup, milk, sour cream, parsley and pepper; spoon over stuffing. Sprinkle remaining buttered stuffing on top.

Crush remaining stuffing mix; dip pork chops in water and coat with the stuffing crumbs. Place on top. Bake, uncovered, at 350° for 1 hour or until pork chops are tender.

YIELD: 6 servings.

Colorful Kielbasa

SCHELBY THOMPSON, WINTER HAVEN, FLORIDA

PREP: 15 min. **COOK:** 30 min.

1	can (10 ¾ ounces) condensed cream of celery soup, undiluted
1½	cups water
1	tablespoon butter
1	pound smoked kielbasa *or* Polish sausage, cut into ½-inch pieces
¾	cup uncooked long grain rice
1	package (10 ounces) frozen peas
1	jar (4½ ounces) sliced mushrooms, drained
1	cup (4 ounces) shredded cheddar cheese

In a large skillet, combine the soup, water and butter; bring to a boil. Add kielbasa and rice. Reduce heat; cover and simmer for about 18 minutes or until rice is almost tender.

Stir in peas and mushrooms. Cover and simmer for 15 minutes or until rice is tender and peas are heated through. Sprinkle with cheese; cover and let stand until cheese is melted.

YIELD: 4-6 servings.

SCALLOPED HAM AND CABBAGE

RUTH PETERSON, JENISON, MICHIGAN

PREP: 15 min. **COOK:** 35 min.

2	cups cubed fully cooked ham
1/2	cup uncooked long grain rice
1/4	cup chopped onion
1/4	cup butter
1 1/2	cups milk
1	can (10 3/4 ounces) condensed cream of mushroom soup, undiluted
1	teaspoon prepared horseradish
1/2	teaspoon salt
3	to 4 cups chopped cabbage

In a large skillet, saute the ham, rice and onion in butter until rice is golden brown and onion is tender.

Stir in the milk, soup, horseradish and salt. Add cabbage; cover and cook over low heat for 35-45 minutes or until the cabbage is tender, stirring occasionally.

YIELD: 4-6 servings.

LAZY PIEROGI BAKE

SANDY STARKS, AMHERST, NEW YORK

PREP: 25 min. **BAKE:** 35 min.

1	package (16 ounces) spiral pasta
1	pound sliced bacon, diced
2	medium onions, chopped
2	garlic cloves, minced
1/2	pound fresh mushrooms, sliced
2	cans (14 ounces *each*) sauerkraut, rinsed and well drained
3	cans (10 3/4 ounces *each*) condensed cream of mushroom soup, undiluted
1/2	cup milk
1/2	teaspoon celery seed
1/8	teaspoon pepper

Cook pasta according to package directions. Meanwhile, in a skillet, cook bacon over medium heat until crisp. Using a slotted spoon, remove to paper towels; drain, reserving 2 tablespoons drippings.

In the drippings, saute onions and garlic until tender. Add mushrooms; cook until tender. Stir in sauerkraut and half of the bacon. In a bowl, combine the soup, milk, celery seed and pepper. Drain pasta.

Place a fourth of the pasta in two greased 13-in. x 9-in. x 2-in. baking dishes. Top each with a fourth of the sauerkraut and soup mixture. Repeat layers.

Cover and bake at 350° for 25 minutes. Uncover; sprinkle with remaining bacon. Bake 10-15 minutes longer or until heated through. Let stand for 5-10 minutes before serving.

YIELD: 16 servings.

OVEN JAMBALAYA

RUBY WILLIAMS, BOGALUSA, LOUISIANA

PREP: 10 min. **BAKE:** 1 hour

2 1/4	cups water
1 1/2	cups uncooked long grain rice
1	can (10 3/4 ounces) condensed cream of celery soup, undiluted
1	can (10 3/4 ounces) condensed cream of onion soup, undiluted
1	can (10 ounces) diced tomatoes and green chilies, undrained
1	pound fully cooked smoked sausage, cut into 1/2-inch slices
1	pound cooked medium shrimp, peeled and deveined

In a large bowl, combine the first five ingredients; mix well. Pour into a greased 13-in. x 9-in. x 2-in. baking dish. Cover and bake at 350° for 40 minutes.

Stir in sausage and shrimp. Cover and bake 20-30 minutes longer or until the rice is tender.

YIELD: 8-10 servings.

POULTRY

CHICKEN AND JULIENNED VEGGIES (pictured left)

LOIS CRISSMAN, MANSFIELD, OHIO

PREP/TOTAL TIME: 20 min.

2	boneless skinless chicken breast halves (4 ounces *each*)
2	teaspoons olive oil
1/2	cup plus 2 tablespoons reduced-fat reduced-sodium condensed cream of chicken soup, undiluted
1/4	cup fat-free milk
1/4	teaspoon dried thyme
1/4	teaspoon salt
1/8	teaspoon white pepper
1	medium carrot, julienned
1	cup julienned zucchini
	Hot cooked spaghetti, optional

In a nonstick skillet, brown chicken on each side in oil. In a bowl, combine the soup, milk, thyme, salt and pepper until smooth; pour over chicken. Add carrot. Reduce heat; cover and simmer for 5 minutes, stirring occasionally.

Add zucchini; cover and simmer 5 minutes longer or until chicken is no longer pink. Serve over spaghetti if desired.

YIELD: 2 servings.

TURKEY APPLE POTPIE

PHYLLIS ATHERTON, SOUTH BURLINGTON, VERMONT

PREP: 15 min. **BAKE:** 25 min.

1/4	cup chopped onion
1	tablespoon butter
2	cans (10 3/4 ounces *each*) condensed cream of chicken soup, undiluted
3	cups cubed cooked turkey
1	large tart apple, cubed
1/3	cup raisins
1	teaspoon lemon juice
1/4	teaspoon ground nutmeg
	Pastry for single-crust pie (9 inches)

In a saucepan, saute onion in butter until tender. Add the soup, turkey, apple, raisins, lemon juice and nutmeg; mix well. Spoon into an ungreased 11-in. x 7-in. x 2-in. baking dish.

On a floured surface, roll pastry to fit top of dish. Cut vents in pastry, using a small apple cookie cutter if desired. Place over filling; flute edges. Bake at 425° for 25-30 minutes or until crust is golden brown and filling is bubbly.

YIELD: 6 servings.

Mexican Turkey Roll-Ups

MARLENE MUCKENHIRN, DELANO, MINNESOTA

PREP: 10 min. **BAKE:** 30 min.

2 1/2	cups cubed cooked turkey
1 1/2	cups (12 ounces) sour cream, *divided*
3	teaspoons taco seasoning, *divided*
1	can (10 3/4 ounces) condensed cream of mushroom soup, undiluted, *divided*
1 1/2	cups (6 ounces) shredded cheddar cheese, *divided*
1	small onion, chopped
1/2	cup salsa
1/4	cup sliced ripe olives
10	flour tortillas (6 inches)
	Shredded lettuce
	Chopped tomatoes
	Additional salsa, optional

In a bowl, combine the turkey, 1/2 cup sour cream, 1 1/2 teaspoons taco seasoning, half of the soup, 1 cup cheese, onion, salsa and olives. Place 1/3 cup filling on each tortilla. Roll up and place seam side down in a greased 13-in. x 9-in. x 2-in. baking dish.

Combine remaining sour cream, taco seasoning and soup; pour over tortillas. Cover and bake at 350° for 30 minutes or until heated through. Sprinkle with remaining cheese. Serve with shredded lettuce and chopped tomatoes. Top with additional salsa if desired.

YIELD: 5 servings.

PINEAPPLE CHICKEN CASSEROLE

SUSAN WARREN, NORTH MANCHESTER, INDIANA

PREP/TOTAL TIME: 30 min.

2	cups cubed cooked chicken
1	can (10 3/4 ounces) condensed cream of mushroom soup, undiluted
1	cup pineapple tidbits
2	celery ribs, chopped
1	tablespoon chopped green onion
1	tablespoon soy sauce
1	can (3 ounces) chow mein noodles, *divided*

In a large bowl, combine the first six ingredients. Fold in 1 cup chow mein noodles.

Transfer to a greased shallow 2-qt. baking dish. Sprinkle with remaining noodles. Bake, uncovered, at 350° for 20-25 minutes or until heated through.

YIELD: 4-6 servings.

CAMPFIRE CHICKEN STEW

FLORENCE KREIS, BEACH PARK, ILLINOIS

PREP: 25 min. GRILL: 40 min.

1	broiler/fryer chicken (3 1/2 to 4 pounds), cut up
3	to 4 medium potatoes, peeled and sliced
1	cup thinly sliced carrots
1	medium green pepper, sliced
1	can (10 3/4 ounces) condensed cream of mushroom soup, undiluted
1/4	cup water
1/2	teaspoon salt
1/4	teaspoon pepper

Grill chicken, uncovered, over medium heat for 3 minutes on each side. Place two pieces of chicken each on four pieces of heavy-duty foil (about 18 in. x 12 in.). Divide the potatoes, carrots and green pepper among the four pieces of foil. Top each with 2 tablespoons soup, 1 tablespoon water, salt and pepper. Fold foil around mixture and seal tightly.

Grill, covered, over medium heat for 20 minutes; turn and grill 20-25 minutes longer or until vegetables are tender and chicken juices run clear.

YIELD: 4 servings.

CHICKEN DIVAN

KARREN RASCHEIN, PRAIRIE DU SAC, WISCONSIN

PREP: 10 min. BAKE: 30 min.

1	package (10 ounces) frozen broccoli spears, thawed and drained
3	chicken breast halves, cooked and sliced
1	can (10 3/4 ounces) condensed cream of broccoli soup, undiluted
1/2	cup mayonnaise
1	teaspoon lemon juice
1	teaspoon butter, melted
1/4	cup soft bread crumbs
1/4	cup shredded Swiss cheese

Place broccoli spears in a greased 8-in. square baking dish. Top with chicken. Combine the soup, mayonnaise and lemon juice; spread over chicken. Toss butter and bread crumbs; add cheese. Sprinkle over sauce. Bake, uncovered, at 350° for 30-35 minutes or until bubbly.

YIELD: 4 servings.

EDITOR'S NOTE: Reduced-fat or fat-free mayonnaise is not recommended for this recipe.

CREAMED CHICKEN IN PASTRY SHELLS

DONA GLOVER, ROCKWALL, TEXAS

PREP: 20 min. **BAKE:** 20 min.

- 2 packages (10 ounces *each*) frozen pastry shells
- 2 celery ribs, finely chopped
- 1 medium onion, chopped
- 2 tablespoons chopped green pepper
- 6 tablespoons butter, *divided*
- 6 tablespoons all-purpose flour
- 1/2 teaspoon salt
- 3 cups milk
- 1 can (10 3/4 ounces) condensed cream of mushroom soup, undiluted
- 4 cups cubed cooked chicken
- 1 can (4 ounces) mushroom stems and pieces, drained
- 1 jar (2 ounces) diced pimientos, drained
- 1/2 cup grated Parmesan cheese
- 1/2 cup sliced almonds

Bake pastry shells according to package directions. Meanwhile, in a skillet, saute the celery, onion and green pepper in 1 tablespoon butter for 10 minutes or until tender. Remove from the heat and set aside.

In a large saucepan, melt the remaining butter over medium heat. Stir in flour and salt until smooth. Gradually add the milk. Bring to a boil; cook and stir for 2 minutes or until thickened. Stir in soup until blended. Add the chicken, mushrooms, pimientos and sauteed vegetables; mix well.

Transfer to a greased 3-qt. baking dish. Sprinkle with Parmesan cheese and almonds. Bake, uncovered, at 350° for 20-25 minutes or until bubbly. Spoon into pastry shells.

YIELD: 6 servings (2 shells each).

COOKING TIP

If you don't have pastry shells, just toast 2 slices of bread per serving. Cut each slice in half diagonally, then arrange on plate and spoon the creamed chicken over the toast.

WILD WILD RICE

LISA NEU, FOND DU LAC, WISCONSIN

PREP: 30 min. **BAKE:** 35 min.

- 1/4 cup chopped green pepper
- 1/4 cup chopped onion
- 2 tablespoons butter, *divided*
- 2 1/3 cups water
- 1 package (6 ounces) long grain and wild rice mix
- 4 cups cubed cooked chicken
- 1 can (10 3/4 ounces) condensed cream of chicken soup, undiluted
- 1 can (8 ounces) French-style green beans, drained
- 1 can (8 ounces) sliced water chestnuts, drained
- 1 medium carrot, grated
- 1/4 cup mayonnaise
- 1 cup (4 ounces) shredded cheddar cheese, optional

In a small skillet, saute green pepper and onion in 1 tablespoon butter until crisp-tender; set aside.

In a large saucepan, bring the water, rice and remaining butter to a boil. Reduce heat; cover and simmer for 25 minutes or until rice is tender. Stir in the chicken, soup, green beans, water chestnuts, carrot, mayonnaise and green pepper mixture.

Transfer to a greased 2 1/2-qt. baking dish. Sprinkle with cheese if desired. Cover and bake at 350° for 35-40 minutes or until heated through.

YIELD: 6-8 servings.

EDITOR'S NOTE: Reduced-fat or fat-free mayonnaise is not recommended for this recipe.

CHICKEN CRESCENT WREATH

MARLENE DENISSEN, MAPLEWOOD, MINNESOTA

PREP: 15 min. **BAKE:** 20 min.

- 2 tubes (8 ounces *each*) refrigerated crescent rolls
- 1 cup (4 ounces) shredded Colby-Monterey Jack cheese
- 2/3 cup condensed cream of chicken soup
- 1/2 cup chopped fresh broccoli
- 1/2 cup chopped sweet red pepper
- 1/4 cup chopped water chestnuts
- 1 can (5 ounces) white chicken, drained *or* 3/4 cup cubed cooked chicken
- 2 tablespoons chopped onion

Unroll crescent roll dough and separate into triangles. Place triangles on a 12-in. pizza pan, forming a ring with pointed ends facing outer edge of pan and wide ends overlapping. Lightly press wide ends together.

Combine the remaining ingredients. Spoon over wide ends of ring. Fold points over filling and tuck under wide ends (filling will be visible). Bake at 375°; for 20-25 minutes or until golden brown.

YIELD: 6-8 servings.

CURRIED CHICKEN WITH ASPARAGUS

MIRIAM CHRISTOPHEL, BATTLE CREEK, MICHIGAN

PREP: 20 min. **BAKE:** 25 min.

1	can (10 ¾ ounces) condensed cream of chicken soup, undiluted
⅓	cup mayonnaise
1	teaspoon lemon juice
½	teaspoon curry powder
⅛	teaspoon pepper
1	package (10 ounces) frozen asparagus spears, thawed
1	pound boneless skinless chicken breasts, cut into ½-inch pieces
2	tablespoons vegetable oil
¼	cup shredded cheddar cheese

In a bowl, combine the soup, mayonnaise, lemon juice, curry and pepper; set aside. Place half of the asparagus in a greased 8-in. square baking dish. Spread with half of the soup mixture.

In a skillet, saute chicken in oil until no longer pink. Place chicken over soup mixture. Top with remaining asparagus and soup mixture.

Cover and bake at 375° for 20 minutes. Uncover; sprinkle with cheese. Bake 5-8 minutes longer or until cheese is melted.

YIELD: 4 servings.

EDITOR'S NOTE: Reduced-fat or fat-free mayonnaise is not recommended for this recipe.

TURKEY STUFFING ROLL-UPS

DARLENE WARD, HOT SPRINGS, ARKANSAS

PREP: 15 min. **BAKE:** 25 min.

1	package (6 ounces) stuffing mix
1	can (10 ¾ ounces) condensed cream of chicken soup, undiluted
¾	cup milk
1	pound sliced deli smoked turkey
1	can (2.8 ounces) french-fried onions, crushed

Prepare the stuffing mix according to package directions. Meanwhile, in a bowl, combine the soup and milk; set aside. Spoon about ¼ cup of the stuffing onto each turkey slice. Roll up.

Place turkey rolls in a greased 13-in. x 9-in. x 2-in. baking dish. Pour soup mixture over roll-ups. Bake, uncovered, at 350° for 20 minutes. Sprinkle with onions. Bake 5 minutes longer or until heated through.

YIELD: 6 servings.

EDITOR'S NOTE: 3 cups of any prepared stuffing can be substituted for the stuffing mix.

BROCCOLI-CHICKEN CUPS

SHIRLEY GERBER, ROANOKE, ILLINOIS

PREP: 15 min. **BAKE:** 20 min.

2	tubes (10 ounces *each*) refrigerated biscuits
2	cups (8 ounces) shredded cheddar cheese, *divided*
1 1/3	cups crisp rice cereal
1	cup cubed cooked chicken
1	can (10 3/4 ounces) condensed cream of mushroom soup, undiluted
1	package (10 ounces) frozen chopped broccoli, cooked and drained

Place biscuits in greased muffin cups, pressing dough over the bottom and up the sides. Add 1 tablespoon cheese and cereal to each cup.

Combine the chicken, soup and broccoli; spoon into cups. Bake at 375° for 20-25 minutes or until bubbly. Sprinkle with remaining cheese.

YIELD: 10-12 servings.

CASHEW CHICKEN CASSEROLE

JULIE RIDLON, SOLWAY, MINNESOTA

PREP: 15 min. + chilling **BAKE:** 35 min.

2	cups uncooked elbow macaroni
3	cups cubed cooked chicken
1/2	cup cubed process cheese (Velveeta)
1	small onion, chopped
1/2	cup chopped celery
1/2	cup chopped green pepper
1	can (8 ounces) sliced water chestnuts, drained
1	can (10 3/4 ounces) condensed cream of mushroom soup, undiluted
1	can (10 3/4 ounces) condensed cream of chicken soup, undiluted
1 1/3	cups milk
1	can (14 1/2 ounces) chicken broth
1/4	cup butter, melted
2/3	cup crushed saltines (about 20 crackers)
3/4	cup cashew halves

In a greased 13-in. x 9-in. x 2-in. baking dish, layer the first seven ingredients in the order listed. In a bowl, combine the soups, milk and broth. Pour over water chestnuts. Cover and refrigerate overnight.

Remove from the refrigerator 30 minutes before baking. Toss butter and cracker crumbs; sprinkle over top, then sprinkle with cashews. Bake, uncovered, at 350° for 35-40 minutes or until macaroni is tender.

YIELD: 6 servings.

CHICKEN PIZZAS

DOROTHY NEAR, COWANSVILLE, QUEBEC

PREP: 20 min. + rising BAKE: 20 min.

CRUST:

1	package (1/4 ounce) active dry yeast
1	cup warm water (110° to 115°)
2 3/4	to 3 cups all-purpose flour
1	tablespoon vegetable oil
1	tablespoon sugar
1/2	teaspoon salt

TOPPING:

1	can (10 3/4 ounces) condensed cream of mushroom soup, undiluted
1	teaspoon paprika
1	teaspoon dried oregano
1/2	teaspoon garlic powder
1/2	teaspoon salt
1/4	teaspoon pepper
1	medium green pepper, chopped
1	small onion, chopped
1/2	pound fresh mushrooms, sliced
1	cup diced cooked chicken
1 1/2	cups (6 ounces) shredded cheddar cheese
2 1/2	cups (10 ounces) shredded part-skim mozzarella cheese

In a large mixing bowl, dissolve yeast in warm water. Add 1 1/2 cups flour, oil, sugar and salt; beat until smooth. Stir in enough remaining flour to form a soft dough.

Turn onto a floured board; knead until smooth and elastic, about 6-8 minutes. Place in a greased bowl, turning once to grease top. Cover and let rise in a warm place until doubled, about 1 hour.

Punch dough down. Divide in half and roll each half into a 13-in. circle. Place each piece on a lightly greased 12- to 14-in. pizza pan.

Combine the soup, paprika, oregano, garlic powder, salt and pepper; spread over each pizza. Layer with the green pepper, onion, mushrooms and chicken. Combine cheeses; sprinkle over pizzas.

Bake at 425° for 20-25 minutes or until crust is browned and cheese is melted.

YIELD: 12-16 servings (2 pizzas).

STUFFED PASTA SHELLS

JUDY MEMO, NEW CASTLE, PENNSYLVANIA

PREP: 15 min. BAKE: 30 min.

1 1/2	cups cooked stuffing
2	cups diced cooked chicken *or* turkey
1/2	cup frozen peas, thawed
1/2	cup mayonnaise
18	jumbo pasta shells, cooked and drained
1	can (10 3/4 ounces) condensed cream of chicken soup, undiluted
2/3	cup water
	Paprika
	Minced fresh parsley

Combine the stuffing, chicken, peas and mayonnaise; spoon into pasta shells. Place in a greased 13-in. x 9-in. x 2-in. baking dish. Combine soup and water; pour over shells. Sprinkle with paprika. Cover and bake at 350° for 30 minutes or until heated through. Sprinkle with parsley.

YIELD: 6 servings.

EDITOR'S NOTE: Reduced-fat or fat-free mayonnaise is not recommended for this recipe.

Place asparagus in a greased 11-in. x 7-in. x 2-in. baking dish; set aside. Sprinkle chicken with salt and pepper. In a large skillet, saute chicken in butter for 10-14 minutes or until juices run clear. Place over asparagus.

Combine the soup, mayonnaise, lemon juice, curry powder, ginger and pepper; spoon over chicken. Bake, uncovered, at 350° for 35 minutes. Sprinkle with almonds. Bake 5 minutes longer or until heated through.

YIELD: 6 servings.

EDITOR'S NOTE: Reduced-fat or fat-free mayonnaise is not recommended for this recipe.

CHICKEN-MUSHROOM LOAF

PEARL ALTMAN, SPRING CHURCH, PENNSYLVANIA

PREP: 10 min. **BAKE:** 50 min. + standing

- 1   can (10 ¾ ounces) condensed cream of mushroom soup, undiluted
- ⅔   cup milk
- 2   eggs, lightly beaten
- 3   cups cubed cooked chicken
- 1   cup cooked rice
- 1   cup dry bread crumbs
- 1   jar (2 ounces) chopped pimientos, drained
- 1   teaspoon onion salt, optional
- 1   teaspoon celery seed
- ½   teaspoon salt, optional
- ½   teaspoon paprika
- ¼   teaspoon pepper

In a large bowl, combine the soup, milk and eggs. Add all remaining ingredients and mix well.

Pour into a greased 8-in. x 4-in. x 2-in. loaf pan. Bake, uncovered, at 325° for 50-55 minutes. Let stand for 10 minutes before cutting.

YIELD: 6 servings.

LEMON-CURRY CHICKEN CASSEROLE

SUE YAEGER, BROOKINGS, SOUTH DAKOTA

PREP: 20 min. **BAKE:** 40 min.

- 2   packages (12 ounces *each*) frozen cut asparagus, thawed and drained
- 4   boneless skinless chicken breast halves, cut into ½-inch strips
-    Salt and pepper to taste
- 3   tablespoons butter
- 1   can (10 ¾ ounces) condensed cream of chicken soup, undiluted
- ½   cup mayonnaise
- ¼   cup lemon juice
- 1   teaspoon curry powder
- ¼   teaspoon ground ginger
- ⅛   teaspoon pepper
- ½   cup sliced almonds, toasted

Turkey Tenderloin Supreme

NANCY LEVIN, CHESTERFIELD, MISSOURI

PREP/TOTAL TIME: 25 min.

- 1 package (20 ounces) turkey breast tenderloins, cut into 1-inch slices
- 1 tablespoon butter
- 1/3 cup chopped green onions
- 1 can (10 3/4 ounces) condensed cream of chicken soup, undiluted
- 1/4 cup water

In a large skillet, brown the turkey in butter. Add onions; cook for 1-2 minutes. Combine the soup and water; pour over turkey. Bring to a boil. Reduce heat; cover and simmer for 8-10 minutes or until meat juices run clear.

YIELD: 4 servings.

Cooking Tip

About 3 green onions— white and green portions— will equal 1/3 cup chopped.

Poppy Seed Chicken

ERNESTINE PLASEK, HOUSTON, TEXAS

PREP: 15 min. **BAKE:** 20 min.

8	ounces sliced fresh mushrooms
1	tablespoon butter
5	cups cubed cooked chicken
1	can (10 ¾ ounces) condensed cream of chicken soup, undiluted
1	cup (8 ounces) sour cream
1	jar (2 ounces) pimientos, drained and diced

TOPPING:

½	cup butter, melted
1⅓	cups finely crushed butter-flavored crackers
2	teaspoons poppy seeds

In a large skillet, saute mushrooms in butter until tender. Stir in the chicken, soup, sour cream and pimientos; mix well.

Transfer to a greased shallow 2-qt. baking dish. In a small bowl, combine all topping ingredients. Sprinkle over the chicken. Bake, uncovered, at 350° for 20 minutes or until heated through.

YIELD: 6 servings.

Firefighter's Chicken Spaghetti

KRISTA DAVIS-KEITH, NEW CASTLE, INDIANA

PREP: 20 min. **BAKE:** 45 min.

12	ounces uncooked spaghetti, broken in half
1	can (10 ¾ ounces) condensed cream of chicken soup, undiluted
1	can (10 ¾ ounces) condensed cream of mushroom soup, undiluted
1	cup (8 ounces) sour cream
½	cup milk
¼	cup butter, melted, *divided*
2	tablespoons dried parsley flakes
½	teaspoon garlic powder
½	teaspoon salt
¼	teaspoon pepper
2	cups (8 ounces) shredded part-skim mozzarella cheese
1	cup grated Parmesan cheese
2	to 3 celery ribs, chopped
1	medium onion, chopped
1	can (4 ounces) mushroom stems and pieces, drained
5	cups cubed cooked chicken
1½	cups crushed cornflakes

Cook spaghetti according to package directions; drain. In a large bowl, combine the soups, soup cream, milk, 2 tablespoons butter and seasonings. Add the cheeses, celery, onion and mushrooms. Stir in the chicken and spaghetti.

Transfer to a greased 3-qt. baking dish (dish will be full). Combine the cornflakes and remaining butter; sprinkle over top. Bake, uncovered, at 350° for 45-50 minutes or until bubbly.

YIELD: 12-14 servings.

SAUCY CHICKEN AND ASPARAGUS

Vicki Schlechter, Davis, California

PREP: 10 min. **BAKE:** 40 min.

1 1/2	pounds fresh asparagus spears, halved
4	boneless skinless chicken breast halves
2	tablespoons vegetable oil
1/2	teaspoon salt
1/4	teaspoon pepper
1	can (10 3/4 ounces) condensed cream of chicken soup, undiluted
1/2	cup mayonnaise
1	teaspoon lemon juice
1/2	teaspoon curry powder
1	cup (4 ounces) shredded cheddar cheese

If desired, partially cook asparagus; drain. Place the asparagus in a greased 9-in. square baking dish.

In a skillet, brown the chicken on each side in oil over medium heat. Season with salt and pepper. Arrange chicken over asparagus. In a bowl, combine the soup, mayonnaise, lemon juice and curry powder; pour over chicken.

Cover and bake at 375° for 40 minutes or until the chicken is tender and juices run clear. Sprinkle with cheese. Let stand for 5 minutes before serving.

YIELD: 4 servings.

EDITOR'S NOTE: Reduced-fat or fat-free mayonnaise is not recommended for this recipe.

Chicken Veggie-Potato Bake

BONNIE SMITH, GOSHEN, INDIANA

PREP: 10 min. **BAKE:** 1 hour

3	cups cubed cooked chicken
4	medium carrots, cut into chunks
3	medium red potatoes, cut into chunks
3	celery ribs, sliced
1	can (10 3/4 ounces) condensed cream of chicken soup, undiluted
2/3	cup water
1/2	teaspoon salt
1/4	teaspoon pepper

Place chicken in a greased shallow 2-qt. baking dish. Top with carrots, potatoes and celery. Combine the soup, water, salt and pepper; pour over vegetables. Cover and bake at 350° for 60-75 minutes or until vegetables are tender.

YIELD: **5 servings.**

HOME-STYLE COOKING WITH CREAM SOUP | **POULTRY**

ONION-TOPPED CHICKEN

KAY FAUST, DEERWOOD, MINNESOTA

PREP: 10 min. **BAKE:** 1 hr. 25 min.

4	boneless skinless chicken breast halves
4	medium potatoes, peeled and halved
1	can (10 3/4 ounces) condensed cream of chicken soup, undiluted
1	cup (8 ounces) sour cream
1	can (2.8 ounces) french-fried onions

Place chicken in a greased 9-in. square baking dish. Arrange potatoes around chicken. Combine soup and sour cream; spread over chicken and potatoes.

Bake, uncovered, at 350° for 1 1/4 hours. Sprinkle with onions; bake 10 minutes longer.

YIELD: 4 servings.

FLAVORFUL FRYER CHICKEN

MARSHA MURRAY, NIVERVILLE, MANITOBA

PREP: 5 min. **BAKE:** 1 hour

1	broiler/fryer chicken (3 to 4 pounds), cut up
1	can (10 3/4 ounces) condensed cream of mushroom soup, undiluted
1	cup orange juice
2	tablespoons onion soup mix
	Hot mashed potatoes *or* cooked rice

Place chicken in a greased 13-in. x 9-in. x 2-in. baking dish. Combine the soup, orange juice and soup mix; pour over chicken.

Cover and bake at 350° for 45 minutes. Uncover; bake 15-20 minutes longer or until chicken juices run clear. Serve over potatoes or rice.

YIELD: 6 servings.

GREEN BEAN CASSEROLE WITH BISCUITS

SANDRA WANAMAKER, GERMANSVILLE, PENNSYLVANIA

PREP: 10 min. **BAKE:** 50 min.

1	can (10 3/4 ounces) condensed cream of chicken soup, undiluted
1	can (10 3/4 ounces) condensed cheddar cheese soup, undiluted
1	can (5 ounces) evaporated milk
3	cups diced cooked chicken
3	cups frozen green beans, thawed and drained
1	cup chopped celery
2	tablespoons chopped onion
1	jar (2 ounces) diced pimientos, drained
1/2	cup chow mein noodles
1/2	cup slivered almonds, toasted
1/2	teaspoon salt
1/4	teaspoon pepper
1/2	cup french-fried onions
	Hot biscuits

In a large bowl, combine soups and milk until smooth. Add the chicken, vegetables, pimientos, noodles, almonds, salt and pepper.

Spoon into a greased shallow 2 1/2-qt. baking dish. Bake, uncovered, at 350° for 40 minutes or until bubbly. Sprinkle with onions; bake 10 minutes longer. Serve over biscuits.

YIELD: 4-6 servings.

LIGHT CHICKEN CORDON BLEU

SHANNON STRATE, SALT LAKE CITY, UTAH

PREP: 20 min. **BAKE:** 25 min.

8	boneless skinless chicken breast halves (4 ounces *each*)
1/2	teaspoon pepper
8	slices (1 ounce *each*) lean deli ham
1 1/2	cups (6 ounces) shredded part-skim mozzarella cheese
2/3	cup fat-free milk
1	cup crushed cornflakes
1	teaspoon paprika
1/2	teaspoon garlic powder
1/4	teaspoon salt

SAUCE:

1	can (10 3/4 ounces) reduced-fat reduced-sodium condensed cream of chicken soup, undiluted
1/2	cup fat-free sour cream
1	teaspoon lemon juice

Flatten chicken to 1/4-in. thickness. Sprinkle with pepper; place a ham slice and 3 tablespoons of cheese down the center of each piece. Roll up and tuck in ends; secure with toothpicks. Pour milk into a shallow bowl. In another bowl, combine the cornflakes, paprika, garlic powder and salt. Dip chicken in milk, then roll in crumbs.

Place in a 13-in. x 9-in. x 2-in. baking dish coated with nonstick cooking spray. Bake, uncovered, at 350° for 25-30 minutes or until juices run clear.

Meanwhile, in a small saucepan, whisk the soup, sour cream and lemon juice until blended; heat through. Discard toothpicks from chicken; serve with sauce.

YIELD: 8 servings.

COOKING TIP

To flatten chicken, cover with a piece of plastic wrap and pound from the center out with the flat side of a meat mallet.

TURKEY SPINACH CASSEROLE

BECCA BRANSFIELD, BURNS, TENNESSEE

PREP: 20 min. **BAKE:** 40 min.

- 1 can (10 ¾ ounces) reduced-fat reduced-sodium condensed cream of chicken soup, undiluted
- ½ cup reduced-fat mayonnaise
- ½ cup water
- 2 cups cubed cooked turkey breast
- 1 package (10 ounces) frozen chopped spinach, thawed and squeezed dry
- ¾ cup uncooked instant brown rice
- 1 medium yellow summer squash, cubed
- ¼ cup chopped red onion
- 1 teaspoon ground mustard
- ½ teaspoon dried parsley flakes
- ½ teaspoon garlic powder
- ⅛ teaspoon pepper
- ¼ cup Parmesan cheese
- ⅛ teaspoon paprika

In a large bowl, combine the soup, mayonnaise and water. Stir in the turkey, spinach, rice, squash, onion, mustard, parsley, garlic powder and pepper.

Transfer to a shallow 2½-qt. baking dish coated with nonstick cooking spray. Cover and bake at 350° for 35-40 minutes or until rice is tender. Uncover and sprinkle with Parmesan and paprika. Bake 5 minutes longer or until heated through.

YIELD: 6 servings.

CREAMY TOMATO CHICKEN

CHARLENE KALB, CATONSVILLE, MARYLAND

PREP/TOTAL TIME: 20 min.

- 6 boneless skinless chicken breast halves
- 2 tablespoons vegetable oil
- 1 can (14 ½ ounces) Italian diced tomatoes, undrained
- 1 can (10 ¾ ounces) condensed cream of chicken soup, undiluted
- ⅛ teaspoon ground cinnamon
- 6 slices part-skim mozzarella cheese
  Hot cooked noodles

In a large skillet, cook chicken in oil over medium heat until juices run clear. Remove and keep warm. Combine the tomatoes, soup and cinnamon; add to the skillet. Cook and stir until heated through.

Return chicken to the skillet; top with cheese. Cover and heat until the cheese is melted. Serve over noodles.

YIELD: 6 servings.

CHICKEN RICE BALLS

KATY MARTIN, TOLEDO, OREGON

PREP: 20 min. **BAKE:** 25 min.

- 1/2 cup finely chopped celery
- 1/3 cup sliced green onions, *divided*
- 2 tablespoons butter
- 2 tablespoons all-purpose flour
- 1/2 cup chicken broth
- 2 cups cooked rice
- 1 1/2 cups finely chopped cooked chicken
- 1/2 cup shredded cheddar cheese
- 1 egg, lightly beaten
- 1/2 teaspoon salt
- 1/2 teaspoon chili powder
- 1/4 teaspoon poultry seasoning
- 1/2 cup finely crushed cornflakes
- 1 can (10 3/4 ounces) condensed cream of mushroom soup, undiluted
- 1/4 cup milk

In a medium saucepan, saute celery and half of the onions in butter until tender. Stir in flour. Add broth; cook and stir for 2 minutes (mixture will be thick). Stir in the rice, chicken, cheese, egg, salt, chili powder and poultry seasoning until well mixed.

Shape 1/4 cupfuls into balls. Roll each in cornflake crumbs and place in a greased 13-in. x 9-in. x 2-in. baking dish. Bake, uncovered, at 350° for 25-30 minutes.

Meanwhile, in a saucepan, combine the soup, milk and remaining onions. Cook and stir over medium heat until smooth and heated through; serve over balls.

YIELD: 4-6 servings.

SAUCY MUFFIN CUPS

KAREN LEHMAN, ABERDEEN, IDAHO

PREP: 15 min. **BAKE:** 25 min.

- 1 loaf (1 pound) frozen bread dough, thawed *or* 12 dinner roll dough portions
- 2 cups diced cooked chicken
- 1 can (10 3/4 ounces) condensed cream of mushroom soup, undiluted
- 1/4 cup sliced ripe olives, drained
- 1/2 cup sliced frozen carrots, thawed
- 2 tablespoons minced fresh parsley
- 1 teaspoon chicken bouillon granules
- 1/4 teaspoon garlic powder
   Dash pepper
- 1/2 cup shredded sharp cheddar cheese

If using bread dough, punch down and divide into 12 pieces. Flatten each piece or roll into a 6-in. circle. Press circles into bottom and up sides of greased muffin cups.

In a saucepan, combine remaining ingredients except cheese; cook and stir for 5 minutes or until heated through. Spoon into bread cups; sprinkle with cheese. Bake, uncovered, at 350° for 25-30 minutes or until browned.

YIELD: 6 servings.

COOKING TIP

About 1 1/2 pounds of boneless skinless chicken breast will yield about 2 cups cubed cooked chicken.

Chicken Tortilla Casserole

PAMELA HOEKSTRA, HUDSONVILLE, MICHIGAN

PREP: 10 min. **BAKE:** 30 min.

1/2	cup chicken broth
1/2	cup chopped onion
1/4	cup chopped celery
3	cups cubed cooked chicken
10	flour tortillas (6 inches), torn into bite-size pieces
1	can (10 3/4 ounces) condensed cream of chicken soup, undiluted
1	can (4 ounces) chopped green chilies
3/4	cup shredded cheddar cheese, *divided*
3/4	cup shredded Monterey Jack cheese, *divided*
1/2	teaspoon white pepper
1	cup salsa

In a saucepan, bring the broth, onion and celery to a boil. Reduce heat; cover and simmer for 5-7 minutes or until vegetables are tender. Place in a large bowl; add the chicken, tortillas, soup, chilies, 1/2 cup cheddar cheese, 1/2 cup Monterey Jack cheese and pepper.

Transfer to a greased 11-in. x 7-in. x 2-in. baking dish. Top with salsa and remaining cheeses. Bake, uncovered, at 350° for 30-35 minutes or until heated through.

YIELD: 4-6 servings.

CHEDDAR CHICKEN MOSTACCIOLI

MRS. TROY HAWK, SHERIDAN, MISSOURI

PREP: 15 min. **BAKE:** 55 min.

1/2	cup chopped onion
1/2	cup chopped celery
1	tablespoon butter
1	can (10 3/4 ounces) condensed cream of mushroom soup, undiluted
1	can (10 3/4 ounces) condensed cream of chicken soup, undiluted
1/2	cup milk
1	can (4 ounces) mushroom stems and pieces, drained
1	jar (2 ounces) diced pimientos, drained
1/4	cup chopped pimiento-stuffed olives
1	tablespoon Worcestershire sauce
1 1/4	teaspoons garlic salt
1/2	teaspoon *each* dried basil, oregano and pepper
4	cups diced cooked chicken
3	cups mostaccioli, cooked and drained
1 1/4	cups (5 ounces) shredded cheddar cheese, *divided*
1	cup (4 ounces) shredded Swiss cheese

In a saucepan, saute onion and celery in butter until tender. Add the soups, milk, mushrooms, pimientos, olives, Worcestershire sauce and seasonings; mix well. Add the chicken, mostaccioli, 3/4 cup cheddar cheese and the Swiss cheese; toss to mix.

Pour into a greased 13-in. x 9-in. x 2-in. baking dish. Cover and bake at 350° for 40 minutes. Uncover; sprinkle with remaining cheddar. Bake 15 minutes longer or until cheese is melted.

YIELD: 6-8 servings.

CHICKEN BEAN ENCHILADAS

JULIE MOUTRAY, WICHITA, KANSAS

PREP: 15 min. **BAKE:** 35 min.

1	can (16 ounces) refried beans
10	flour tortillas (8 inches)
1	can (10 ¾ ounces) condensed cream of chicken soup, undiluted
1	cup (8 ounces) sour cream
3	to 4 cups cubed cooked chicken
3	cups (12 ounces) shredded cheddar cheese, *divided*
1	can (15 ounces) enchilada sauce
¼	cup sliced green onions
¼	cup sliced ripe olives
	Shredded lettuce, optional

Spread about 2 tablespoons of beans on each tortilla. Combine soup and sour cream; stir in chicken. Spoon ⅓ to ½ cup down the center of each tortilla; top with 1 tablespoon cheese. Roll up and place seam side down in a greased 13-in. x 9-in. x 2-in. baking dish.

Pour enchilada sauce over top; sprinkle with the onions, olives and remaining cheese. Bake, uncovered, at 350° for 35 minutes or until heated through. Just before serving, sprinkle lettuce around enchiladas if desired.

YIELD: 10 servings.

BAKED PHEASANT IN GRAVY

LOU BISHOP, PHILLIPS, WISCONSIN

PREP: 15 min. **BAKE:** 45 min.

½	cup all-purpose flour
½	cup packed brown sugar
6	pheasant *or* grouse breast halves
3	tablespoons butter
1	can (10 ¾ ounces) condensed cream of celery soup, undiluted
1	to 1 ⅓ cups water
1	cup chicken broth
1	can (2.8 ounces) french-fried onions
	Mashed potatoes or hot cooked rice

In a large resealable plastic bag, combine flour and brown sugar; add pheasant pieces, one at time, and shake to coat. In a large skillet, brown pheasant on both sides in butter over medium heat. Transfer to a greased 13-in. x 9-in. x 2-in. baking dish.

Combine the soup, water and broth until blended; pour over pheasant. Bake, uncovered, at 350° for 40 minutes. Sprinkle with onions. Bake 5-10 minutes longer or until juices run clear. Serve with potatoes or rice.

YIELD: 6 servings.

sauce if desired. Pour over chicken. Top each chicken breast with a lemon slice.

Reduce heat; cover and simmer until chicken juices run clear, about 5 minutes. Serve over spaghetti and sprinkle with additional parsley if desired.

YIELD: 4 servings.

CHICKEN IN CREAMY GRAVY

JEAN LITTLE, CHARLOTTE, NORTH CAROLINA

PREP/TOTAL TIME: 25 min.

- 4 boneless skinless chicken breast halves (1 pound)
- 1 tablespoon canola oil
- 1 can (10 3/4 ounces) reduced-fat reduced-sodium condensed cream of chicken *or* broccoli soup, undiluted
- 1/4 cup fat-free milk
- 1 tablespoon minced fresh parsley
- 2 teaspoons lemon juice
- 1/8 teaspoon pepper
- 1/8 teaspoon Worcestershire sauce, optional
- 4 lemon slices
       Hot cooked spaghetti, optional
       Additional minced fresh parsley, optional

In a nonstick skillet, cook chicken in oil until browned on each side, about 10 minutes; drain. In a bowl, combine the soup, milk, parsley, lemon juice, pepper and Worcestershire

CHICKEN MEAL-IN-ONE

JINA NICKEL, LAWTON, OKLAHOMA

PREP: 10 min. **BAKE:** 1 1/4 hours

- 4 1/2 cups frozen shredded hash brown potatoes
- 2 cups frozen cut green beans, thawed
- 1 cup frozen sliced carrots, thawed
- 4 bone-in chicken breasts (6 ounces *each*)
- 1 can (10 3/4 ounces) condensed cream of chicken *or* mushroom soup, undiluted
- 3/4 cup water
- 2 tablespoons dry onion soup mix
       Salt and pepper to taste

In an ungreased 13-in. x 9-in. x 2-in. baking dish, combine the hash browns, beans and carrots. Top with chicken. Combine remaining ingredients; pour over chicken and vegetables.

Cover and bake at 375° for 50 minutes. Uncover; bake 25-30 minutes longer or until chicken juices run clear.

YIELD: 4 servings.

GROUND TURKEY STROGANOFF

JEFF GILL, VALDOSTA, GEORGIA

PREP/TOTAL TIME: 25 min.

- 1   pound ground turkey
- 1   small onion, grated
- 1   cup sliced mushrooms
- 2   cans (10 3/4 ounces *each*) condensed cream of mushroom soup, undiluted
- 1/3 cup buttermilk
- 1   teaspoon garlic powder
- 1/2 teaspoon salt
- 1/4 to 1/2 teaspoon pepper
- 1   cup (8 ounces) sour cream
-      Hot cooked noodles
-      Minced fresh parsley, optional

In a skillet, cook turkey and onion over medium heat until meat is no longer pink; drain. Add mushrooms; cook and stir for 1 minute. Stir in the soup, buttermilk, garlic powder, salt and pepper. Bring to a boil. Reduce heat; simmer, uncovered, for 5-10 minutes.

Stir in sour cream; heat gently but do not boil. Serve over noodles. Garnish with parsley if desired.

YIELD: 4 servings.

COOKING TIP

This stroganoff is just as tasty using ground chicken, lean ground beef or ground pork.

CHICKEN BROCCOLI CASSEROLE

COLLEEN LEWIS, COTTONWOOD, ARIZONA

PREP: 10 min. BAKE: 25 min.

- 3   cups fresh broccoli florets (about 1 1/4 pounds)
- 2   cups cubed cooked chicken *or* turkey
- 1   can (10 3/4 ounces) condensed cream of chicken soup, undiluted
- 1/2 cup mayonnaise
- 1/2 cup grated Parmesan cheese
- 1/2 teaspoon curry powder
- 1   cup cubed fresh bread
- 2   tablespoons butter, melted

Place broccoli and 1 in. of water in a large saucepan. Bring to a boil. Reduce heat; cover and simmer for 5-8 minutes or until crisp-tender. Drain and place in a greased 11-in. x 7-in. x 2-in. baking dish.

Combine the chicken, soup, mayonnaise, Parmesan cheese and curry powder; spoon over broccoli. Top with bread cubes and butter. Bake, uncovered, at 350° for 25-30 minutes or until heated through.

YIELD: 6 servings.

EDITOR'S NOTE: Reduced-fat or fat-free mayonnaise is not recommended for this recipe.

ALMOND BACON CHICKEN

RUTH PETERSON, JENISON, MICHIGAN

PREP/TOTAL TIME: 30 min.

4	bacon strips
4	boneless skinless chicken breast halves
1/4	teaspoon pepper
1	can (10 3/4 ounces) condensed cream of onion soup, undiluted
1/4	cup chicken broth
1/4	cup sliced almonds, toasted

Place bacon on a microwave-safe plate lined with microwave-safe paper towels. Cover with another paper towel; microwave on high for 1-3 minutes or until partially cooked. Wrap a bacon strip around each chicken breast. Sprinkle with pepper. Arrange in an 8-in. square microwave-safe dish. Cover and microwave on high for 7 minutes; drain.

In a bowl, combine soup and broth; cover and microwave for 2 minutes. Spoon around chicken. Cook, uncovered, 5-7 minutes longer or until juices run clear. Let stand for 5 minutes before serving. Sprinkle with almonds.

YIELD: 4 servings.

EDITOR'S NOTE: This recipe was tested in an 850-watt microwave oven.

TURKEY NOODLE CASSEROLE

GEORGIA HENNINGS, ALLIANCE, NEBRASKA

PREP: 30 min. BAKE: 30 min.

2	pounds ground turkey
2	cups chopped celery
1/4	cup chopped green pepper
1/4	cup chopped onion
1	can (10 3/4 ounces) condensed cream of mushroom soup, undiluted
1	can (8 ounces) sliced water chestnuts, drained
1	jar (4 1/2 ounces) sliced mushrooms, drained
1	jar (4 ounces) diced pimientos, drained
1/4	cup soy sauce
1/2	teaspoon salt
1/2	teaspoon lemon-pepper seasoning
1	cup (8 ounces) sour cream
8	ounces wide egg noodles, cooked and drained

In a large skillet, cook the turkey, celery, green pepper and onion over medium heat until meat is no longer pink and vegetables are tender. Stir in the soup, water chestnuts, mushrooms, pimientos, soy sauce, salt and lemon-pepper. Bring to a boil. Reduce heat; simmer, uncovered, for 20 minutes.

Remove from the heat; add sour cream and noodles. Spoon half into a freezer container; cover and freeze for up to 3 months. Place remaining mixture in a greased shallow 2-qt. baking dish. Cover and bake at 350° for 30-35 minutes or until heated through.

TO USE FROZEN CASSEROLE: Thaw in the refrigerator. Transfer to a greased 2-qt. baking dish and bake as directed.

YIELD: 2 casseroles (6 servings each).

LATTICE CHICKEN POTPIE

ANGIE COTTRELL, SUN PRAIRIE, WISCONSIN

PREP: 10 min. BAKE: 35 min.

- 1 package (16 ounces) frozen California-blend vegetables
- 2 cups cubed cooked chicken
- 1 can (10 3/4 ounces) condensed cream of potato soup, undiluted
- 1 cup milk
- 1 cup (4 ounces) shredded cheddar cheese
- 1 can (2.8 ounces) french-fried onions
- 1/2 teaspoon seasoned salt
- 1 tube (8 ounces) refrigerated crescent rolls

In a large bowl, combine the vegetables, chicken, soup, milk, cheese, onions and seasoned salt. Transfer to a greased 13-in. x 9-in. x 2-in. baking dish.

Unroll the crescent roll dough and separate into two rectangles. Seal perforations; cut each rectangle lengthwise into 1/2-in. strips. Form a lattice crust over the chicken mixture. Bake, uncovered, at 375° for 35-40 minutes or until golden brown.

YIELD: 4-6 servings.

1/3	cup seasoned bread crumbs
2	tablespoons butter, melted
1	to 2 tablespoons grated Parmesan cheese

Cook fettuccine according to package directions. Meanwhile, in a Dutch oven, combine the soup, cream cheese, mushrooms, cream, butter and garlic powder. Add the cheeses; cook and stir until cheese is melted. Add chicken; heat through. Drain fettuccine; add to the sauce.

Transfer to a greased shallow 2 1/2-qt. baking dish. Combine topping ingredients; sprinkle over chicken mixture. Cover and bake at 350° for 25 minutes. Uncover; bake 5-10 minutes longer or until golden brown.

YIELD: 6-8 servings.

FOUR-CHEESE CHICKEN FETTUCCINE

ROCHELLE BROWNLEE, BIG TIMBER, MONTANA

PREP: 20 min. **BAKE:** 30 min.

8	ounces uncooked fettuccine
1	can (10 3/4 ounces) condensed cream of mushroom soup, undiluted
1	package (8 ounces) cream cheese, cubed
1	jar (4 1/2 ounces) sliced mushrooms, drained
1	cup heavy whipping cream
1/2	cup butter
1/4	teaspoon garlic powder
3/4	cup grated Parmesan cheese
1/2	cup shredded part-skim mozzarella cheese
1/2	cup shredded Swiss cheese
2 1/2	cups cubed cooked chicken

CRUNCHY TURKEY CASSEROLE

LOIS KOOGLER, SIDNEY, OHIO

PREP: 15 min. **BAKE:** 30 min.

2	cans (10 3/4 ounces *each*) condensed cream of mushroom soup, undiluted
1/2	cup milk *or* chicken broth
4	cups cubed cooked turkey
2	celery ribs, thinly sliced
1	small onion, chopped
1	can (8 ounces) sliced water chestnuts, drained and halved
1	tablespoon soy sauce
1	can (3 ounces) chow mein noodles
1/2	cup slivered almonds

In a large bowl, combine soup and milk. Stir in the turkey, celery, onion, water chestnuts and soy sauce.

Transfer to a greased shallow 2-qt. baking dish. Sprinkle with noodles and almonds. Bake, uncovered, at 350° for 30 minutes or until heated through.

YIELD: 6-8 servings.

Twisty Pasta Primavera with Chicken

ELAINE ANDERSON, ALIQUIPPA, PENNSYLVANIA

PREP/TOTAL TIME: 25 min.

2	quarts water
2 1/2	cups uncooked spiral pasta
2	cups chopped broccoli
3/4	cup sliced carrots
1	cup (4 ounces) shredded part-skim mozzarella cheese
2	cups cubed cooked chicken breast
1	can (10 3/4 ounces) reduced-fat reduced-sodium condensed cream of broccoli soup, undiluted
1	cup fat-free milk
1/4	cup grated Parmesan cheese
1/8	teaspoon garlic powder
1/8	teaspoon pepper

In a large saucepan, bring water to a boil. Add pasta; cook for 4 minutes. Add broccoli and carrots; cook 4-5 minutes longer or until pasta is tender. Drain and place in a bowl. Add mozzarella cheese and chicken.

In another saucepan, combine the remaining ingredients. Bring to a boil; cook and stir until blended. Pour over pasta mixture and toss gently. Serve immediately.

YIELD: 6 servings.

Easy Chicken Enchiladas

CHERYL POMRENKE, COFFEYVILLE, KANSAS

PREP: 15 min. **BAKE:** 25 min. + standing

3	cups (12 ounces) shredded cheddar cheese, *divided*
2	cups (8 ounces) shredded Monterey Jack cheese
2	cups chopped cooked chicken
2	cups (16 ounces) sour cream
1	can (10 3/4 ounces) condensed cream of chicken soup, undiluted
1	can (4 ounces) chopped green chilies
2	tablespoons finely chopped onion
1/4	teaspoon pepper
1/8	teaspoon salt
10	flour tortillas (8 inches), warmed

In a large bowl, combine 2 cups cheddar cheese, Monterey Jack cheese, chicken, sour cream, soup, chilies, onion, pepper and salt. Spoon about 1/2 cup off center on each tortilla; roll up. Place seam side down in a greased 13-in. x 9-in. x 2-in. baking dish.

Cover and bake at 350° for 20 minutes. Uncover; sprinkle with remaining cheddar cheese. Bake 5 minutes longer or until cheese is melted. Let stand for 10 minutes before serving.

YIELD: 8 servings.

FARMHOUSE CHICKEN

ALICE FAYE ELLIS, ELKTON, OREGON

PREP: 10 min. **BAKE:** 30 min.

- 2 packages (6 ounces *each*) stuffing mix
- 4 cups cubed cooked chicken
- 2 cans (10 3/4 ounces *each*) condensed cream of celery soup, undiluted
- 1 cup milk
- 2 celery ribs, chopped
- 1 teaspoon dried minced onion
- 1/4 teaspoon salt
- 1/4 teaspoon pepper

Prepare stuffing mix according to package directions; set aside. Place the chicken in a greased 13-in. x 9-in. x 2-in. baking dish. Combine the soup, milk, celery, onion, salt and pepper until blended; pour over chicken. Top with stuffing. Bake, uncovered, at 350° for 30-35 minutes or until bubbly.

YIELD: 8 servings.

CREAMY CHICKEN 'N' RICE

RENEE LEETCH, CANTON, OHIO

PREP/TOTAL TIME: 10 min.

- 1 cup instant rice
- 1 cup water
- 1 can (15 ounces) mixed vegetables, drained
- 1 can (10 3/4 ounces) condensed cream of chicken soup, undiluted
- 1 can (5 ounces) chunk white chicken, drained
- 1/4 to 1/2 teaspoon dried basil
  Pinch pepper

In a saucepan, cook rice in water according to package directions. Add the remaining ingredients; heat through.

YIELD: 4 servings.

TURKEY POTATO MEATBALLS

KATHY RUSERT, MENA, ARKANSAS

PREP: 20 min. **BAKE:** 30 min.

- 2 medium potatoes, peeled and shredded
- 2 medium carrots, grated
- 1 small onion, grated
- 1/2 cup dry bread crumbs
- 1/4 cup egg substitute
- 1/8 teaspoon pepper
- 1 1/2 pounds ground turkey
- 1 tablespoon vegetable oil
- 1 can (10 3/4 ounces) reduced-fat reduced-sodium condensed cream of mushroom soup, undiluted
- 1 1/3 cups fat-free milk
- 1/2 cup uncooked instant rice

In a large bowl, combine the potatoes, carrots, onion, bread crumbs, egg substitute and pepper. Crumble turkey over mixture and mix well. Shape into 1-in. balls.

In a skillet, brown meatballs in batches in oil; set aside. In an ungreased 13-in. x 9-in. x 2-in. baking dish, combine soup, milk and rice; stir in meatballs. Cover and bake at 350° for 30-35 minutes or until meatballs are no longer pink.

YIELD: 10 servings.

CALIFORNIA CHICKEN CASSEROLE

DEBBIE KOKES, TABOR, SOUTH DAKOTA

PREP: 10 min. **BAKE:** 45 min.

1	can (10 ¾ ounces) condensed cream of mushroom soup, undiluted
⅓	cup milk
1	package (16 ounces) frozen California-blend vegetables, thawed
1½	cups cubed cooked chicken
1½	cups (6 ounces) shredded Swiss cheese, *divided*
1	jar (2 ounces) diced pimientos, drained
	Salt and pepper to taste
	Hot cooked rice

In a bowl, combine soup and milk. Stir in the vegetables, chicken, 1¼ cups cheese, pimientos, salt and pepper.

Transfer to a greased 9-in. square baking dish. Cover and bake at 350° for 40 minutes. Uncover; top with remaining cheese. Bake 5-10 minutes longer or until bubbly. Let stand for 5 minutes. Serve over rice.

YIELD: 4 servings.

SOUR CREAM 'N' DILL CHICKEN

REBEKAH BROWN, THREE HILLS, ALBERTA

PREP: 10 min. **BAKE:** 1 hour

8	to 10 chicken pieces, skin removed
	Pepper to taste
1	can (10 ¾ ounces) condensed cream of mushroom soup, undiluted
1	envelope onion soup mix
1	cup (8 ounces) sour cream
1	tablespoon lemon juice
1	tablespoon fresh dill, chopped *or* 1 teaspoon dill weed
1	can (4 ounces) sliced mushrooms, drained
	Paprika
	Cooked wide egg noodles, optional

Place chicken in a single layer in a 13-in. x 9-in. x 2-in. baking dish. Sprinkle with pepper. Combine the soup, soup mix, sour cream, lemon juice, dill and mushrooms; pour over chicken. Sprinkle with paprika.

Bake, uncovered, at 350° for 1 hour or until chicken is tender. Serve over egg noodles if desired.

YIELD: 4-6 servings.

Turkey Sausage Casserole

NANCY ARNOLD, JOHNSON CITY, TENNESSEE

PREP: 15 min. BAKE: 20 min.

1	package (10 ounces) spiral noodles
1/2	cup finely chopped onion
2	teaspoons butter, *divided*
1	pound smoked turkey sausage, cut into 1/4-inch slices
1/2	pound fresh mushrooms, sliced
1	can (10 3/4 ounces) reduced-fat reduced-sodium condensed cream of chicken soup, undiluted
1	can (10 3/4 ounces) condensed cheddar cheese soup, undiluted
1	cup fat-free evaporated milk
1/2	cup crushed reduced-fat butter-flavored crackers

Cook noodles according to package directions; drain. In a skillet, saute onion in 1 teaspoon butter until tender. Stir in the noodles, sausage, mushrooms, soups and milk.

Transfer to a 13-in. x 9-in. x 2-in. baking dish coated with nonstick cooking spray. Sprinkle with cracker crumbs; dot with remaining butter. Bake, uncovered, at 375° for 20-25 minutes or until heated through.

YIELD: 8 servings.

Cumin Chicken With Apples

RAYMONDE BOURGEOIS, SWASTIKA, ONTARIO

PREP: 20 min. BAKE: 1 hour

4	chicken legs with thighs
2	tablespoons butter
2	medium apples, chopped
2	small onions, halved and sliced
1	can (4 1/2 ounces) mushroom stems and pieces, drained
1	tablespoon all-purpose flour
1	can (10 3/4 ounces) condensed cream of mushroom soup, undiluted
1/2	cup water
1	tablespoon ground cumin
1	teaspoon Worcestershire sauce
3/4	teaspoon salt
1/4	teaspoon pepper
1/4	teaspoon chili powder
	Hot cooked rice

In a large skillet, brown chicken in butter. Transfer to a greased 13-in. x 9-in. x 2-in. baking dish. In the drippings, saute the apples, onions and mushrooms until apples are crisp-tender. Add the flour, soup, water, cumin, Worcestershire sauce, salt and pepper; mix well. Pour over chicken.

Cover and bake at 350° for 1 hour or until the chicken juices run clear. Sprinkle with the chili powder. Serve over the rice.

YIELD: 4 servings.

In a large bowl, combine the soup, mayonnaise and lemon juice. Add the chicken, onion, peppers, $1/2$ cup Monterey Jack cheese and $1/2$ cup of cheddar cheese; mix well. Add noodles and toss to coat.

Transfer to a greased shallow 2-qt. baking dish. Bake, uncovered, at 350° for 30-35 minutes. Sprinkle with remaining cheeses. Bake 10 minutes longer or until vegetables are tender and cheese is melted.

YIELD: 6 servings.

EDITOR'S NOTE: Reduced-fat or fat-free mayonnaise is not recommended for this recipe.

WHITE TURKEY CHILI

TINA BARRETT, HOUSTON, TEXAS

PREP/TOTAL TIME: 30 min.

2	cups cubed cooked turkey breast
2	cans (15 ounces *each*) white kidney *or* cannellini beans, rinsed and drained
1	can (10 $3/4$ ounces) reduced-fat reduced-sodium condensed cream of chicken soup, undiluted
1 $1/3$	cups fat-free milk
1	can (4 ounces) chopped green chilies, drained
1	tablespoon dried minced onion
1	tablespoon minced fresh cilantro
1	teaspoon garlic powder
1	teaspoon ground cumin
1	teaspoon dried oregano
6	tablespoons fat-free sour cream

In a large saucepan, combine the first 10 ingredients; bring to a boil. Reduce heat; cover and simmer for 25-30 minutes or until heated through. Garnish with sour cream.

YIELD: 6 servings.

CHICKEN NOODLE CASSEROLE

KAY PEDERSON, YELLVILLE, ARKANSAS

PREP: 15 min. **BAKE:** 40 min.

1	can (10 $3/4$ ounces) condensed cream of chicken soup, undiluted
$1/2$	cup mayonnaise
2	tablespoons lemon juice
2	cups cubed cooked chicken
1	small onion, chopped
$1/4$	cup chopped green pepper
$1/4$	cup chopped sweet red pepper
1	cup (4 ounces) shredded Monterey Jack cheese, *divided*
1	cup (4 ounces) shredded sharp cheddar cheese, *divided*
12	ounces medium egg noodles, cooked and drained

SKILLET CHICKEN AND VEGETABLES

ANNETTE PHILLIPS, BATON ROUGE, LOUISIANA

PREP: 20 min. COOK: 40 min.

1	broiler-fryer chicken (3 1/2 to 4 pounds), cut up
2	tablespoons vegetable oil
1	cup sliced onion
1	can (10 3/4 ounces) condensed cream of celery soup, undiluted
2	tablespoons Worcestershire sauce
1/2	to 1 teaspoon salt
1/2	teaspoon dried oregano
2	cups sliced zucchini
1	package (10 ounces) frozen green beans, thawed

In a large skillet, brown chicken in oil, a few pieces at a time; remove from skillet and set aside. Discard all but 2 teaspoons drippings. Saute onion in drippings until tender. Add the soup, Worcestershire sauce, salt and oregano; stir until smooth.

Return chicken to skillet; bring to a boil. Reduce heat; cover and simmer for 30-40 minutes. Add zucchini and green beans; cover and simmer for 10 minutes or until chicken juices run clear.

YIELD: 4 servings.

CHICKEN LASAGNA

JANET LORTON, EFFINGHAM, ILLINOIS

PREP: 20 min. BAKE: 35 min. + standing

9	uncooked lasagna noodles
2	cans (10 3/4 ounces *each*) condensed cream of chicken soup, undiluted
2/3	cup milk
2 1/2	cups frozen mixed vegetables
2	cups cubed cooked chicken
18	slices process American cheese

Cook noodles according to package directions; drain. In a large saucepan, combine soup and milk. Cook and stir over low heat until blended. Remove from the heat; stir in vegetables and chicken.

In a greased 13-in. x 9-in. x 2-in. baking dish, layer three noodles, a third of the soup mixture and six cheese slices. Repeat layers twice.

Cover and bake at 350° for 30 minutes. Uncover; bake 5-10 minutes longer or until bubbly. Let stand for 15 minutes before cutting.

YIELD: 9-12 servings.

Cordon Bleu Casserole

COLLEEN BAKER, WONEWOC, WISCONSIN

PREP: 10 min. **BAKE:** 50 min.

6	slices whole wheat bread
6	chicken breast halves, cooked and sliced
1	package (8 ounces) cream cheese, thinly sliced
1/2	pound sliced fully cooked ham
1 1/2	cups (6 ounces) shredded Swiss cheese, *divided*
2	packages (10 ounces *each*) frozen broccoli spears, thawed and drained
2	cans (10 3/4 ounces *each*) condensed cream of chicken soup, undiluted
1/4	teaspoon pepper

Place bread in the bottom of a greased 13-in. x 9-in. x 2-in. baking dish. Layer with the chicken, cream cheese slices and ham. Sprinkle with 1 cup Swiss cheese. Top with broccoli.

Combine soup and pepper; spoon over broccoli. Sprinkle with remaining Swiss cheese. Bake, uncovered, at 350° for 50-55 minutes or until bubbly.

YIELD: 8-10 servings.

Turkey Biscuit Potpie

SHIRLEY FRANCEY, ST. CATHARINES, ONTARIO

PREP: 30 min. **BAKE:** 20 min.

1	large onion, chopped
1	garlic clove, minced
1 1/2	cups cubed peeled potatoes
1 1/2	cups sliced carrots
1	cup frozen cut green beans, thawed
1	cup reduced-sodium chicken broth
4 1/2	teaspoons all-purpose flour
1	can (10 3/4 ounces) reduced-fat condensed cream of mushroom soup, undiluted
2	cups cubed cooked turkey
2	tablespoons minced fresh parsley
1/2	teaspoon dried basil
1/2	teaspoon dried thyme
1/4	teaspoon pepper

BISCUITS:

1	cup all-purpose flour
2	teaspoons baking powder
1/2	teaspoon dried oregano
2	tablespoons cold butter
7	tablespoons 1% milk

In a large saucepan coated with nonstick cooking spray, cook onion and garlic over medium heat until tender. Add the potatoes, carrots, beans and broth; bring to a boil. Reduce heat; cover and simmer for 15-20 minutes or until potatoes are tender.

Remove from the heat. Combine the flour and soup; stir into vegetable mixture. Add the turkey and seasonings. Transfer to a shallow 2-qt. baking dish coated with nonstick cooking spray.

In a bowl, combine the flour, baking powder and oregano. Cut in the butter until evenly distributed. Stir in milk. Drop batter in six mounds onto hot turkey mixture. Bake, uncovered, at 400° for 20-25 minutes or until a toothpick inserted in center of biscuits comes out clean and biscuits are golden brown.

YIELD: 6 servings.

Chicken Tetrazzini

MARTHA SUE STROUD, CLARKSVILLE, TEXAS

PREP: 15 min. **BAKE:** 1 hour

- 1 package (16 ounces) uncooked spaghetti
- 1 medium green pepper, chopped
- 1 medium onion, chopped
- 2 tablespoons butter
- 2 cups cubed cooked chicken
- 2 cans (4 ounces *each*) mushrooms, drained
- 1 jar (2 ounces) diced pimientos, drained
- 1 can (10 ¾ ounces) condensed cream of mushrooms soup, undiluted
- 2 cups milk
- ½ teaspoon garlic powder
- ½ teaspoon salt
- 1 to 1 ½ cups (4 to 6 ounces) shredded cheddar cheese

Cook spaghetti according to package directions. Meanwhile, in a large Dutch oven; saute green pepper and onion in butter until peppers are crisp-tender. Stir in the chicken, mushrooms, pimientos, soup, milk, garlic powder and salt. Drain spaghetti and add to mixture; toss.

Pour into a greased 13-in. x 9-in. x 2-in. baking dish. Bake, uncovered, at 350° for 50-60 minutes or until hot and bubbly. Sprinkle with cheese; bake 10 minutes longer or until the cheese is melted.

YIELD: 10-12 servings.

ROTINI CHICKEN CASSEROLE

MRS. RUTH LEE, TROY, ONTARIO

PREP: 15 min. **BAKE:** 35 min.

2 ¾	cups uncooked tricolor rotini *or* spiral pasta
¾	cup chopped onion
½	cup chopped celery
2	garlic cloves, minced
1	tablespoon olive oil
3	cups cubed cooked chicken breast
1	can (10 ¾ ounces) reduced-fat reduced-sodium condensed cream of chicken soup, undiluted
1 ½	cups fat-free milk
1	package (16 ounces) frozen Italian-blend vegetables
1	cup (4 ounces) shredded reduced-fat cheddar cheese
2	tablespoons minced fresh parsley
1 ¼	teaspoons dried thyme
1	teaspoon salt
⅔	cup crushed cornflakes

Cook pasta according to package directions. Meanwhile, in a nonstick skillet, saute the onion, celery and garlic in oil until tender. Drain pasta; place in a bowl. Add the onion mixture, chicken, soup, milk, frozen vegetables, cheese, parsley, thyme and salt.

Pour into a shallow 3-qt. baking dish coated with nonstick cooking spray. Cover and bake at 350° for 25 minutes. Uncover; sprinkle with cornflakes, then spray with non-stick cooking spray. Bake 10-15 minutes longer or until heated through.

YIELD: 8 servings.

COMFORTING CHICKEN

EDNA THOMAS, WARSAW, INDIANA

PREP: 15 min. **BAKE:** 55 min.

- 1   pound boneless skinless chicken breasts, cut into cubes
- 1/2   cup finely chopped onion
- 1/2   cup finely chopped green pepper
- 1   tablespoon vegetable oil
- 1   tablespoon butter
- 1   can (10 3/4 ounces) condensed cream of mushroom soup, undiluted
- 1   cup water
- 3/4   cup uncooked long grain rice
- 1/2   teaspoon salt
- 1/2   teaspoon chili powder
- 1/4   teaspoon pepper
- 1/4   teaspoon paprika

In a large skillet, cook and stir the chicken, onion and green pepper in oil and butter until the chicken is lightly browned and vegetables are tender. Stir in the remaining ingredients.

Transfer to a lightly greased shallow 1 1/2-qt. baking dish. Cover and bake at 375° for 55-60 minutes or until the rice is tender.

YIELD: 4 servings.

TURKEY NOODLE STEW

TRACI MALONEY, TOMS RIVER, NEW JERSEY

PREP/TOTAL TIME: 30 min.

- 2   turkey breast tenderloins (about 1/2 pound *each*), cut into 1/4-inch slices
- 1   medium onion, chopped
- 1   tablespoon vegetable oil
- 1   can (14 1/2 ounces) chicken broth
- 1   can (10 3/4 ounces) condensed cream of celery soup, undiluted
- 2   cups frozen mixed vegetables
- 1/2   to 1 teaspoon lemon-pepper seasoning
- 3   cups uncooked extra-wide egg noodles

In a large skillet, cook turkey and onion in oil until turkey is no longer pink, about 6 minutes; drain. Combine the broth, soup, vegetables and lemon-pepper. Add to the skillet; bring to a boil. Stir in noodles. Reduce heat; cover and simmer for 10 minutes or until noodles and vegetables are tender.

YIELD: 6 servings.

Prepare rice according to package directions; place in a large bowl. Dissolve bouillon in hot water; add to rice. Stir in the turkey, celery, soup, water chestnuts, mushrooms, onion and soy sauce.

Transfer to a greased 3-qt. baking dish. Toss bread crumbs and butter; sprinkle over the top. Bake, uncovered, at 350° for 55-60 minutes or until heated through.

YIELD: 8 servings.

Corn Bread Chicken Bake

MADGE BRITTON, AFTON, TENNESSEE

PREP: 20 min. **BAKE:** 45 min.

1 1/4	pounds boneless skinless chicken breasts
6	cups cubed corn bread
8	bread slices, cubed
1	medium onion, chopped
2	cans (10 3/4 ounces *each*) condensed cream of chicken soup, undiluted
1	cup chicken broth
2	tablespoons butter, melted
1 1/2	to 2 teaspoons rubbed sage
1	teaspoon salt
1/2	to 1 teaspoon pepper

Place chicken in a large skillet and cover with water; bring to a boil. Reduce heat; cover and simmer for 12-14 minutes or until juices run clear. Drain and cut into cubes.

In a large bowl, combine the remaining ingredients. Add chicken. Transfer to a greased 13-in. x 9-in. x 2-in. baking dish. Bake, uncovered, at 350° for 45 minutes or until heated through.

YIELD: 8-10 servings.

Wild Turkey Rice Bake

MARGARET HILL, ROANOKE, VIRGINIA

PREP: 40 min. **BAKE:** 55 min.

1	package (6 ounces) long grain and wild rice mix
1	teaspoon chicken bouillon granules
1	cup hot water
3 1/2	cups cubed fully cooked wild turkey *or* domestic turkey
1 1/2	cups chopped celery
1	can (10 3/4 ounces) condensed cream of mushroom soup, undiluted
1	can (8 ounces) sliced water chestnuts, drained
1	jar (6 ounces) sliced mushrooms, drained
1/2	cup chopped onion
1/4	cup soy sauce
1	cup soft bread crumbs
2	tablespoons butter, melted

ARTICHOKE CHICKEN

ROBERTA GREEN, HEMET, CALIFORNIA

PREP: 10 min. **BAKE:** 30 min.

2	cans (14 ounces *each*) water-packed artichoke hearts, drained and quartered
2	tablespoons olive oil
3	garlic cloves, minced
2 2/3	cups cubed cooked chicken
2	cans (10 3/4 ounces *each*) condensed cream of chicken soup, undiluted
1	cup mayonnaise
1	teaspoon lemon juice
1/2	teaspoon curry powder
1 1/2	cups (6 ounces) shredded cheddar cheese
1	cup seasoned bread crumbs
1/4	cup grated Parmesan cheese
2	tablespoons butter, melted

In a bowl, combine the artichokes, oil and garlic. Place in a greased shallow 2 1/2-qt. baking dish. Top with chicken.

Combine the soup, mayonnaise, lemon juice and curry; pour over the chicken. Sprinkle with cheddar cheese. Combine the bread crumbs, Parmesan cheese and butter; sprinkle over top. Bake, uncovered, at 350° for 30-35 minutes or until bubbly.

YIELD: **6-8 servings.**

EDITOR'S NOTE: Reduced-fat or fat-free mayonnaise is not recommended for this recipe.

BAKED SWISS CHICKEN

BEVERLY ROBERGE, BRISTOL, CONNECTICUT

PREP: 5 min. **BAKE:** 35 min.

6	boneless skinless chicken breast halves (1 1/2 pounds)
1	can (10 3/4 ounces) condensed cream of chicken soup, undiluted
1/2	cup white wine *or* chicken broth
6	slices Swiss cheese
1	cup crushed seasoned croutons

Place chicken in a greased 13-in. x 9-in. x 2-in. baking dish. In a bowl, combine the soup and wine or broth; pour over chicken. Top with cheese and sprinkle with croutons. Bake, uncovered, at 350° for 35-40 minutes or until chicken juices run clear.

YIELD: **6 servings.**

SEAFOOD

TUNA IN THE STRAW CASSEROLE (pictured left)

KALLEE MCCREERY, ESCONDIDO, CALIFORNIA

PREP/TOTAL TIME: 30 min.

- 1 can (10 3/4 ounces) condensed cream of mushroom soup, undiluted
- 1 can (5 ounces) evaporated milk
- 1 can (6 ounces) tuna, drained and flaked
- 1 can (4 ounces) mushroom stems and pieces, drained
- 1 cup frozen mixed vegetables, thawed
- 2 cups potato sticks, *divided*

In a bowl, combine the soup and milk until blended. Stir in the tuna, mushrooms, vegetables and 1 1/2 cups potato sticks.

Transfer to a greased shallow 1 1/2-qt. baking dish. Bake, uncovered, at 375° for 20 minutes. Sprinkle with the remaining potatoes. Bake 5-10 minutes longer or until bubbly and potatoes are crisp.

YIELD: 4 servings.

SHRIMP NEWBURG

DONNA SOUDERS, HAGERSTOWN, MARYLAND

PREP/TOTAL TIME: 15 min.

- 1 can (10 3/4 ounces) condensed cream of shrimp *or* mushroom soup, undiluted
- 1/4 cup water
- 1 teaspoon seafood seasoning
- 1 package (1 pound) frozen cooked medium salad shrimp, thawed
   Hot cooked rice

In a saucepan, combine the soup, water and seafood seasonings. Bring to boil. Reduce heat; stir in shrimp. Heat through. Serve over rice.

YIELD: 4 servings.

STUFFED HADDOCK

JEANNETTE WOJTOWICZ, BUFFALO, NEW YORK

PREP: 15 min. **BAKE:** 25 min.

1	tablespoon chopped onion
1	tablespoon butter
5	butter-flavored crackers, crushed
1	haddock, sole *or* cod fillet (about 1 pound)
1/3	cup condensed cream of celery soup, undiluted
1	tablespoon sour cream
	Paprika

In a skillet, saute onion in butter until tender. Stir in crackers and enough water to hold mixture together.

Cut a pocket into side of fillet; stuff with cracker mixture. Place in a greased baking dish. Combine soup and sour cream; spread over fish. Sprinkle with paprika. Bake, uncovered, at 350° for 25-30 minutes or until fish flakes easily with a fork.

YIELD: 2 servings.

COOKING TIP

When buying fresh fish, look for firm fish that is elastic to the touch, is moist looking and has a mild aroma.

SEAFOOD LASAGNA

VIOLA WALMER, TEQUESTA, FLORIDA

PREP: 15 min. **BAKE:** 50 min. + standing

3/4	cup chopped onion
2	tablespoons butter
1	package (8 ounces) cream cheese, cubed
1 1/2	cups (12 ounces) small-curd cottage cheese
1	egg, beaten
2	teaspoons dried basil
1	teaspoon salt
1/4	teaspoon pepper
1	can (10 3/4 ounces) condensed cream of shrimp soup, undiluted
1	can (10 3/4 ounces) condensed cream of mushroom soup, undiluted
1/2	cup white wine *or* chicken broth
1/2	cup milk
2	packages (8 ounces *each*) imitation crabmeat, flaked
1	can (6 ounces) small shrimp, rinsed and drained
9	lasagna noodles, cooked and drained
1/2	cup grated Parmesan cheese
3/4	cup shredded Monterey Jack cheese

In a large skillet, saute onion in butter until tender. Reduce heat. Add cream cheese; cook and stir until melted and smooth. Stir in the cottage cheese, egg, basil, salt and pepper. Remove from the heat and set aside. In a bowl, combine the soups, wine or broth, milk, crab and shrimp.

Arrange three noodles in a greased 13-in. x 9-in. x 2-in. baking dish. Spread with a third of cottage cheese mixture and a third of the seafood mixture. Repeat layers twice. Sprinkle with Parmesan cheese.

Cover and bake at 350° for 40 minutes. Uncover; sprinkle with Monterey Jack cheese. Bake 10 minutes longer or until cheese is melted and lasagna is bubbly. Let stand for 15 minutes before cutting.

YIELD: 12 servings.

CORN BREAD-TOPPED SALMON

BILLIE WILSON, MURRAY, KENTUCKY

PREP: 15 min. **BAKE:** 30 min.

2	cans (10 3/4 ounces *each*) condensed cream of mushroom soup, undiluted
1/4	cup milk
1	can (14 3/4 ounces) salmon, drained, bones and skin removed
1 1/2	cups frozen peas, thawed
1	package (8 1/2 ounces) corn bread/muffin mix
1	jar (4 ounces) diced pimientos, drained
1/4	cup finely chopped green pepper
1	teaspoon finely chopped onion
1/2	teaspoon celery seed
1/4	teaspoon dried thyme

In a large saucepan, bring the soup and milk to a boil. Add salmon and peas. Pour into a greased shallow 2 1/2-qt. baking dish.

Prepare corn bread batter according to package directions; stir in the remaining ingredients. Spoon over salmon mixture.

Bake, uncovered, at 400° for 30-35 minutes or until a toothpick inserted in the corn bread comes out clean.

YIELD: 6-8 servings.

Tuna Bake with Cheese Swirls

VIRGINIA MAGEE, REENE, NEW HAMPSHIRE

PREP: 30 min. **BAKE:** 20 min.

- 3 tablespoons chopped onion
- 3 tablespoons chopped green pepper
- 1/3 cup butter
- 1/3 cup all-purpose flour
- 3 cups milk
- 1 can (10 3/4 ounces) condensed cream of mushroom soup, undiluted
- 1 can (12 ounces) tuna, drained and flaked
- 1 tablespoon lemon juice
- 1 teaspoon salt

DOUGH:
- 2 cups biscuit/baking mix
- 1/2 cup milk
- 1/2 cup shredded cheddar cheese

- 1/2 cup diced pimientos
- 1/4 cup minced fresh parsley
- 1 egg
- 2 teaspoons water

In a saucepan, saute onion and green pepper in butter. Blend in flour until smooth. Gradually stir in milk. Bring to a boil over medium heat; cook and stir for 2 minutes or until thickened. Remove from the heat; stir in the soup, tuna, lemon juice and salt. Pour into an ungreased 13-in. x 9-in. x 2-in. baking dish.

For dough, combine biscuit mix and milk until blended. On a lightly floured surface, roll dough into a 12-in. x 9-in. rectangle. Sprinkle with cheese, pimientos and parsley. Roll up jelly-roll style, starting with a long side. Cut into 1-in. slices; place over tuna mixture. Beat egg and water; brush over the swirls. Bake, uncovered, at 400° for 20-25 minutes or until top is lightly browned.

YIELD: 6-8 servings.

Curried Shrimp

SUE FRIEND, LYNDEN, WASHINGTON

PREP/TOTAL TIME: 15 min.

- 1 small onion, chopped
- 1 tablespoon vegetable oil
- 1 can (10 3/4 ounces) condensed cream of shrimp soup, undiluted
- 1 teaspoon curry powder
- 1 package (1 pound) frozen uncooked small shrimp, thawed, peeled and deveined
- 1 cup (8 ounces) sour cream
  Hot cooked rice

In a large saucepan, saute onion in oil until tender. Stir in soup and curry powder; bring to a boil. Add the shrimp; cook and stir until shrimp turn pink. Reduce heat. Stir in sour cream; heat through. Serve over rice.

YIELD: 4 servings.

Quick Crab Mornay

GENEVA SCHMIDTKA, CANANDAIGUA, NEW YORK

PREP/TOTAL TIME: 30 min.

1   can (10 3/4 ounces) condensed cream
      of chicken soup, undiluted

1/3   cup white wine *or* chicken broth

1   egg, lightly beaten

1   can (6 ounces) crabmeat, drained,
      flaked and cartilage removed

1/2   cup shredded cheddar cheese

In a small saucepan, combine soup and wine or broth. Cook and stir over medium heat until blended and heated through. Stir 1/2 cupful into the egg; return all to the pan, stirring constantly.

Place the crab in a greased shallow 1-qt. baking dish; top with soup mixture. Sprinkle with cheese. Bake, uncovered, at 350° for 20 minutes or until the top is lightly browned and cheese is melted.

YIELD: 4-6 servings.

Catch-of-the-Day Casserole

CATHY CLUGSTON, CLOVERDALE, INDIANA

PREP: 15 min. **BAKE:** 30 min.

4   ounces small shell pasta

1   can (10 3/4 ounces) condensed cream
      of celery soup, undiluted

1/2   cup mayonnaise

1/4   cup milk

1/4   cup shredded cheddar cheese

1   package (10 ounces) frozen peas,
      thawed

1   can (7 1/2 ounces) salmon, drained,
      bones and skin removed

1   tablespoon finely chopped onion

Cook pasta according to package directions. Meanwhile, in a bowl, combine the soup, mayonnaise, milk and cheese. Stir in the peas, salmon and onion. Drain pasta; add to salmon mixture.

Transfer to a greased shallow 2-qt. baking dish. Bake, uncovered, at 350° for 30-35 minutes or until bubbly.

YIELD: 4 servings.

EDITOR'S NOTE: Reduced-fat or fat-free mayonnaise is not recommended for this recipe.

CREAMED CRAB ON TOAST

NINA DE WITT, AURORA, OHIO

PREP/TOTAL TIME: 10 min.

- 1   can (10 ¾ ounces) condensed cream of mushroom soup, undiluted
- 1   can (6 ounces) crabmeat, rinsed, drained, and cartilage removed
- 1   tablespoon lemon juice
- ¼   teaspoon dried marjoram
      Dash cayenne pepper
      Toast *or* biscuits

In a 1-qt. microwave-safe dish, combine the soup, crab, lemon juice, marjoram and cayenne. Cover and microwave on high for 3-4 minutes or until heated through, stirring once. Serve on toast or biscuits.

YIELD: 4 servings.

EDITOR'S NOTE: This recipe was tested in a 1,100-watt microwave.

SHRIMP CHICKEN SKILLET

KELLY CORRIGAN, CRAWFORDVILLE, FLORIDA

PREP/TOTAL TIME: 20 min.

- ½   pound fresh mushrooms, sliced
- ¼   cup butter
- ½   cup sliced green onions
- 2   cans (10 ¾ ounces *each*) condensed cream of chicken soup, undiluted
- ½   cup half-and-half cream
- ¼   cup chicken broth
- ¼   cup sherry *or* additional chicken broth
- 1   cup (4 ounces) shredded cheddar cheese
- 2   cups cubed cooked chicken
- 2   cups cooked medium shrimp, peeled and deveined
- 2   tablespoons minced fresh parsley
      Hot cooked rice

In a large skillet, saute mushrooms in butter for 5 minutes. Add onions; saute for 3 minutes or until tender. Stir in the soup, cream, broth and sherry or additional broth. Cook and stir over medium-low heat until blended; add cheese, stirring until melted. Add the chicken, shrimp and parsley; heat through. Serve over rice.

YIELD: 6 servings.

CRUMB-TOPPED HADDOCK

DEBBIE SOLT, LEWISTOWN, PENNSYLVANIA

PREP: 5 min. **BAKE:** 35 min.

- 2   pounds haddock *or* cod fillet
- 1   can (10 ¾ ounces) condensed cream of shrimp soup, undiluted
- 1   teaspoon grated onion
- 1   teaspoon Worcestershire sauce
- 1   cup crushed butter-flavored crackers (about 25 crackers)

Arrange fillet in a greased 13-in. x 9-in. x 2-in. baking dish. Combine the soup, onion and Worcestershire sauce; pour over fish.

Bake, uncovered, at 375° for 20 minutes. Sprinkle with cracker crumbs. Bake 15 minutes longer or until fish flakes easily with a fork.

YIELD: 6-8 servings.

Broccoli Tuna Bake

PAMELA TESORIERO, ETIWANDA, CALIFORNIA

PREP: 10 min. **BAKE:** 30 min.

1	can (10 3/4 ounces) condensed cream of chicken soup, undiluted
1/3	cup milk
1	tablespoon lemon juice
1	can (12 ounces) albacore tuna, drained and flaked
1 1/2	cups cooked rice
1/4	teaspoon pepper
1	package (10 ounces) frozen broccoli florets, cooked and drained
1/2	cup shredded cheddar cheese

In a bowl, combine the soup, milk and lemon juice. Stir in the tuna, rice and pepper.

Transfer to a greased 10-in. pie plate or quiche dish. Bake, uncovered, at 375° for 25 minutes. Top with broccoli; sprinkle with cheese. Bake 5-10 minutes longer or until cheese is melted.

YIELD: 4-6 servings.

COOKING TIP

For a different taste, try this recipe with cream of mushroom soup or cream of broccoli soup.

BAKED SHRIMP AND ASPARAGUS

JANE RHODES, SILVERDALE, WASHINGTON

PREP/TOTAL TIME: 30 min.

1	package (12 ounces) frozen cut asparagus
1	pound medium shrimp, peeled and deveined
1	can (10 3/4 ounces) condensed cream of shrimp soup, undiluted
1	tablespoon butter, melted
1	teaspoon soy sauce
1/2	cup salad croutons, optional
	Hot cooked rice

In a large bowl, combine asparagus, shrimp, soup, butter and soy sauce. Spoon into a greased 8-in. square baking dish.

Bake, uncovered, at 425° for 20 minutes or until shrimp turn pink. Top with croutons if desired; bake 5 minutes longer. Serve over rice.

YIELD: 4-6 servings.

BROCCOLI TUNA SQUARES

JANET JUNCKER, GENEVA, OHIO

PREP: 15 min. **BAKE:** 35 min.

1	tube (8 ounces) refrigerated crescent rolls
1	cup (4 ounces) shredded Monterey Jack cheese
1	package (10 ounces) frozen chopped broccoli, cooked and drained
4	eggs
1	can (10 3/4 ounces) condensed cream of broccoli soup, undiluted
2	tablespoons mayonnaise
3/4	teaspoon onion powder
1/2	teaspoon dill weed
1	can (12 ounces) tuna, drained and flaked
1	tablespoon diced pimientos, drained

Unroll crescent roll dough into one long rectangle; place in an ungreased 13-in. x 9-in. x 2-in. baking dish. Seal seams and perforations; press onto bottom and 1/2 in. up the sides.

Sprinkle with cheese and broccoli. In a bowl, combine the eggs, soup, mayonnaise, onion powder and dill. Stir in tuna and pimientos; pour over broccoli.

Bake, uncovered, at 350° for 35-40 minutes or until a knife inserted near the center comes out clean. Let stand for 10 minutes before serving.

YIELD: 8 servings.

SPECIAL SEAFOOD LINGUINE

VALERIE PUTSEY, WINAMAC, INDIANA

PREP: 10 min. COOK: 35 min.

1	large red onion, chopped
1/2	cup chopped green pepper
3	garlic cloves, minced
1/3	cup minced fresh parsley
1/4	cup olive oil
1	can (28 ounces) diced tomatoes, undrained
1	can (10 3/4 ounces) condensed cream of shrimp soup, undiluted
1	tablespoon lemon juice
1	teaspoon dried basil
1	teaspoon dried oregano
1/4	teaspoon salt
1/4	teaspoon pepper
1	pound uncooked medium shrimp, peeled and deveined
2	cans (6 ounces *each*) crabmeat, drained, flaked and cartilage removed
1	package (16 ounces) linguine
1/4	cup shredded Parmesan cheese

In a large skillet, saute the onion, green pepper, garlic and parsley in oil until tender. Add the tomatoes, soup, lemon juice and seasonings. Bring to a boil. Reduce heat; simmer, uncovered, for 20 minutes.

Stir in the shrimp and crab; simmer for 10 minutes or until shrimp turn pink. Meanwhile, cook the linguine according to package directions; drain. Serve seafood mixture over linguine; sprinkle with Parmesan cheese.

YIELD: 6-8 servings.

CREAMY DILL SALMON STEAKS

VALERIE HUTSON, BYRON, MINNESOTA

PREP/TOTAL TIME: 25 min.

1/2	cup chopped green onions
1	tablespoon butter
1	can (10 3/4 ounces) condensed cream of chicken soup, undiluted
1/2	cup half-and-half cream
2	tablespoons white wine *or* chicken broth
2	tablespoons chopped fresh dill *or* 2 teaspoons dill weed
4	salmon steaks (1 inch thick)

In a large skillet, saute the onions in butter. Add the soup, cream, wine or broth and dill. Place salmon steaks on top. Cover and simmer for 15 minutes or until fish flakes easily with a fork.

YIELD: 4 servings.

CREAMY SEAFOOD ENCHILADAS

EVELYN GEBHARDT, KASILOF, ALASKA

PREP: 20 min. **BAKE:** 30 min.

1/4	cup butter
1/4	cup all-purpose flour
1	cup chicken broth
1	can (10 3/4 ounces) condensed cream of chicken soup, undiluted
1	cup (8 ounces) sour cream
1/2	cup salsa
1/8	teaspoon salt
1	cup (8 ounces) small-curd cottage cheese
1	pound small shrimp, cooked, peeled and deveined
1	cup cooked *or* canned crabmeat, drained, flaked and cartilage removed
1 1/2	cups (6 ounces) shredded Monterey Jack cheese
1	can (4 ounces) chopped green chilies
1	tablespoon dried cilantro
12	flour tortillas (7 inches)
	Additional salsa

In a saucepan, melt butter. Stir in flour until smooth; gradually add broth and soup until blended. Bring to a boil; cook and stir for 2 minutes or until slightly thickened. Remove from the heat. Stir in the sour cream, salsa and salt; set aside.

Place cottage cheese in a blender; cover and process until smooth. Transfer to a bowl; add the shrimp, crab, Monterey Jack cheese, chilies and cilantro.

Spread 3/4 cup sauce in a greased 13-in. x 9-in. x 2-in. baking dish. Place about 1/3 cup seafood mixture down the center of each tortilla. Roll up and place seam side down over sauce. Top with the remaining sauce. Bake, uncovered, at 350° for 30-35 minutes or until heated through. Serve with additional salsa.

YIELD: 6 servings.

MUSHROOM HADDOCK LOAF

CRAIG BROWN, SIOUX CITY, IOWA

PREP: 15 min. **BAKE:** 55 min.

1 1/2	cups crushed saltines (about 45 crackers)
1	can (10 3/4 ounces) condensed cream of mushrooms soup, undiluted
2	eggs, lightly beaten
1/3	cup milk
2	tablespoons chopped green onion
1	tablespoon lemon juice
2	drops hot pepper sauce
2	cups flaked cooked haddock

In a bowl, combine the cracker crumbs, soup, eggs, milk, onion, lemon juice and pepper sauce. Add the haddock.

Press into a greased 8-in. x 4-in. x 2-in. loaf pan. Bake, uncovered, at 350° for 55-60 minutes or until a knife inserted near the center comes out clean.

YIELD: 6 servings.

TUNA NOODLE CASSEROLE

RUBY WELLS, CYNTHIANA, KENTUCKY

PREP: 10 min. **BAKE:** 30 min.

1	can (10 3/4 ounces) reduced-fat reduced-sodium condensed cream of celery soup, undiluted
1/2	cup fat-free milk
2	cups cooked yolk-free wide noodles
1	cup frozen peas, thawed
1	can (6 ounces) light water-packed tuna, drained and flaked
1	jar (2 ounces) diced pimientos, drained
2	tablespoons dry bread crumbs
1	tablespoon butter, melted

In a large bowl, combine soup and milk until smooth. Add the noodles, peas, tuna and pimientos; mix well.

Pour into a shallow 1 1/2-qt. baking dish coated with nonstick cooking spray. Bake, uncovered, at 400° for 25 minutes. Toss bread crumbs and butter; sprinkle over the top. Bake 5 minutes longer or until golden brown.

YIELD: 4 servings.

Bayou Country Seafood Casserole

ETHEL MILLER, EUNICE, LOUISIANA

PREP: 35 min. **BAKE:** 30 min.

- 1 medium onion, chopped
- 1 medium green pepper, chopped
- 1 celery rib, chopped
- 1 garlic clove, minced
- 6 tablespoons butter
- 1 can (10 3/4 ounces) condensed cream of mushroom soup, undiluted
- 1 pound uncooked shrimp, peeled and deveined
- 1 1/2 cups cooked rice
- 2 cans (6 ounces *each*) crabmeat, drained, flaked and cartilage removed *or* 1 1/2 pounds cooked crabmeat
- 4 slices day-old bread, cubed
- 3/4 cup half-and-half cream
- 1/4 cup chopped green onion tops
- 1/2 teaspoon salt
- 1/4 teaspoon pepper
- Dash cayenne pepper

TOPPING:
- 2 tablespoons butter, melted
- 1/3 cup dry bread crumbs
- 2 tablespoons snipped fresh parsley

In a large skillet, saute the onion, green pepper, celery and garlic in butter until tender. Add soup and shrimp. Cook and stir over medium heat for 10 minutes or until shrimp turn pink. Stir in the rice, crab, bread cubes, cream, onion tops and seasonings. Spoon into a greased shallow 2-qt. baking dish.

Combine the topping ingredients; sprinkle over shrimp mixture. Bake, uncovered, at 375° for 25-30 minutes or until heated through.

YIELD: 8 servings.

COOKING TIP

Foil pouches of crabmeat are ready to use and don't require removing any cartilage. You can use two pouches for each 6-ounce can of crabmeat.

STUFFED SOLE

WINNIE HIGGINS, SALISBURY, MARYLAND

PREP: 20 min. **BAKE:** 35 min.

- 1   cup chopped onion
- 2   cans (4 1/4 ounces *each*) small shrimp, rinsed and drained
- 1   jar (4 1/2 ounces) sliced mushrooms, drained
- 2   tablespoons butter
- 1/2   pound fresh cooked *or* canned crabmeat, drained and cartilage removed
- 8   sole *or* flounder fillets (2 to 2 1/2 pounds)
- 1/2   teaspoon salt
- 1/4   teaspoon pepper
- 1/4   teaspoon paprika
- 2   cans (10 3/4 ounces *each*) condensed cream of mushroom soup, undiluted
- 1/3   cup chicken broth
- 2   tablespoons water
- 2/3   cup shredded cheddar cheese
- 2   tablespoons minced fresh parsley

  Cooked wild, brown *or* white rice *or* a mixture, optional

In a saucepan, saute the onion, shrimp and mushrooms in butter until onion is tender. Add crab; heat through. Sprinkle fillets with the salt, pepper and paprika. Spoon crab mixture on fillets; roll up and fasten with a toothpick.

Place in a greased 13-in. x 9-in. x 2-in. baking dish. Combine the soup, broth and water until smooth. Pour over fillets. Sprinkle with cheese. Cover and bake at 400° for 30 minutes. Uncover; sprinkle with parsley. Bake 5 minutes longer or until the fish flakes easily with a fork. Serve over rice if desired.

YIELD: 8 servings.

SIDES

POTATOES SUPREME (pictured left)

MRS. AFTON JOHNSON, SUGAR CITY, IDAHO

PREP: 35 min. + cooling **BAKE:** 25 min.

- 8 to 10 medium potatoes, peeled and cubed
- 1 can (10 ¾ ounces) condensed cream of chicken soup, undiluted
- 3 cups (12 ounces) shredded cheddar cheese, *divided*
- 1 cup (8 ounces) sour cream
- 3 green onions, chopped

   Salt and pepper to taste

Place potatoes in a saucepan and cover with water. Bring to a boil; cover and cook until almost tender. Drain and set aside to cool.

Combine the soup, 1 ½ cups cheese, sour cream, onions, salt and pepper; stir in potatoes. Place in a greased 13-in. x 9-in. x 2-in. baking dish. Sprinkle with remaining cheese. Bake, uncovered, at 350° for 25-30 minutes or until heated through.

YIELD: 8-10 servings.

SUMMER SQUASH CASSEROLE

CAROLE DAVIS, KEENE, NEW HAMPSHIRE

PREP: 20 min. **BAKE:** 35 min.

- 18 cups sliced zucchini *or* yellow summer squash (about 6 pounds)
- 6 medium carrots, shredded
- 3 medium onions, chopped
- 1 ½ cups butter, *divided*
- 3 cans (10 ¾ ounces *each*) condensed cream of chicken soup, undiluted
- 3 cups (24 ounces) sour cream
- 3 packages (8 ounces *each*) crushed stuffing mix

In a Dutch oven, saute the squash, carrots and onions in 6 tablespoons butter until tender; remove from the heat. Stir in soup and sour cream. Melt the remaining butter; add to stuffing mix. Gently stir into the squash mixture.

Transfer to two greased 13-in. x 9-in. x 2-in. baking dishes. Bake, uncovered, at 350° for 35-40 minutes or until stuffing is heated through.

YIELD: 26-30 servings.

Festive Green Bean Casserole

JUNE MULLINS, LIVONIA, MISSOURI

PREP/TOTAL TIME: 30 min.

1	cup chopped sweet red pepper
1	small onion, finely chopped
1	tablespoon butter
1	can (10 ¾ ounces) condensed cream of celery soup, undiluted
½	cup milk
1	teaspoon Worcestershire sauce
⅛	teaspoon hot pepper sauce
2	packages (16 ounces *each*) frozen French-style green beans, thawed and drained
1	can (8 ounces) sliced water chestnuts, drained
1	cup (4 ounces) shredded cheddar cheese

In a skillet, saute red pepper and onion in butter until tender. Add the soup, milk, Worcestershire sauce and hot pepper sauce; stir until smooth. Stir in beans and water chestnuts.

Transfer to an ungreased shallow 1½-qt. baking dish. Sprinkle with cheese. Bake, uncovered, at 350° for 15 minutes or until heated through.

YIELD: 6-8 servings.

ASPARAGUS FLORENTINE

TIFFINY TRUMP-HUMBERT, RAUHEIM, GERMANY

PREP: 15 min. **BAKE:** 30 min.

2 1/2   pounds fresh asparagus, trimmed and cut into 1-inch pieces
1   medium onion, chopped
1   garlic clove, minced
1/4   cup butter
1   can (10 3/4 ounces) condensed cream of celery soup, undiluted
1/2   cup water
3   egg yolks
1   tablespoon Worcestershire sauce
1/8   teaspoon ground mustard
Dash pepper
2   tablespoons lemon juice
1   package (8 ounces) cream cheese, cubed
1   package (10 ounces) frozen chopped spinach, thawed and squeezed dry

Place asparagus in a saucepan with a small amount of water; bring to a boil. Reduce heat; cover and simmer for 3-5 minutes or until crisp-tender. Drain and set aside. In a large saucepan, saute onion and garlic in butter until tender.

In a bowl, whisk together the soup, water, egg yolks, Worcestershire sauce, mustard and pepper. Whisk in lemon juice. Add to onion mixture. Add cream cheese. Cook and stir over low heat until cheese is melted. Stir in spinach and asparagus; heat through.

Transfer to a greased 13-in. x 9-in. x 2-in. baking dish. Bake, uncovered, at 325° for 30-35 minutes or until a thermometer reads 160°. Let stand for 5 minutes before serving.

YIELD: 12 servings.

CABBAGE AU GRATIN

LINDA FUNDERBURKE, BROCKPORT, NEW YORK

PREP/TOTAL TIME: 30 min.

1   medium head cabbage, shredded (about 8 cups)
1   can (10 3/4 ounces) condensed cream of celery soup, undiluted
2   tablespoons milk
1   cup shredded process cheese (Velveeta)
1   cup soft bread crumbs
1   tablespoon butter

In a large covered saucepan, cook cabbage in boiling salted water for 5 minutes; drain. Place in a greased 8-in. square baking dish.

In a small saucepan, blend soup and milk; heat through. Reduce heat; add cheese and stir until melted. Pour over cabbage. Saute the bread crumbs in butter until golden; sprinkle over cabbage. Bake, uncovered, at 350° for 15-20 minutes or until heated through.

YIELD: 8-10 servings.

 **COOKING TIP** | Fresh asparagus can be stored in the refrigerator for up to 4 days. To store, wrap cut ends with a damp paper towel and place in a plastic bag.

Spinach Supreme

CYNDI GAVIN, BLACKFOOT, IDAHO

PREP: 10 min. **BAKE:** 25 min.

- 2   packages (10 ounces *each*) frozen chopped spinach, thawed and squeezed dry
- 2   cups (8 ounces) shredded Monterey Jack cheese
- 1   can (10 ¾ ounces) condensed cream of potato soup, undiluted
- 1   cup (8 ounces) sour cream
- ½   cup grated Parmesan cheese

In a large bowl, combine all of the ingredients. Transfer to a greased 11-in. x 7-in. x 2-in. baking dish. Bake, uncovered, at 325° for 25-30 minutes or until edges are lightly browned and bubbly.

YIELD: 4-6 servings.

Corn Vegetable Casserole

ROY AND JERRETTA LOGAN, FERGUSON, MISSOURI

PREP: 20 min. **BAKE:** 35 min.

- 3   cups chopped broccoli
- 2   cups sliced carrots (½ inch thick)
- 1½   cups pearl onions
- 3½   cups fresh corn
- 1   can (10 ¾ ounces) condensed cream of celery soup, undiluted
- ½   cup milk
- 1   tablespoon Worcestershire sauce
- 1   teaspoon garlic powder
- 1½   cups (6 ounces) shredded cheddar cheese, *divided*

In a Dutch oven, bring 6 cups water to a boil. Add carrots; boil for 1 minute. Add broccoli and boil 1 minute longer. Remove with a slotted spoon and immediately place vegetables in ice water. Drain and pat dry.

Add pearl onions to the boiling water; boil for 3 minutes. Drain and rinse in cold water; peel and set aside.

Combine the corn, broccoli, carrots and onions; place in a greased 13-in. x 9-in. x 2-in. baking dish.

In a bowl, combine the soup, milk, Worcestershire sauce and garlic powder. Add 1 cup cheese. Pour over vegetables. Top with remaining cheese. Bake, uncovered, at 350° for 35-40 minutes or until bubbly and heated through.

YIELD: 12 servings.

BRUSSELS SPROUTS IN CHEESE SAUCE

LUCY MEYRING, WALDEN, COLORADO

PREP/TOTAL TIME: 20 min.

1 1/4	pounds fresh brussels sprouts *or* 1 package (18 ounces) frozen brussels sprouts
1	can (10 3/4 ounces) condensed cream of mushroom soup, undiluted
1/4	cup milk
1	cup (4 ounces) shredded sharp cheddar cheese
1/8	teaspoon salt
1/8	teaspoon pepper
1	can (8 ounces) sliced water chestnuts, drained
1/2	cup slivered almonds, toasted

Cook brussels sprouts in boiling water. Meanwhile, in a saucepan over medium heat, combine the soup, milk, cheese, salt and pepper; cook and stir until cheese is melted. Drain brussels sprouts; transfer to a serving dish. Add water chestnuts and cheese sauce. Sprinkle with almonds. Serve immediately.

YIELD: 6-8 servings.

HARVEST CARROTS

MARTY RUMMEL, TROUT LAKE, WASHINGTON

PREP: 15 min. **BAKE:** 30 min.

4	cups sliced carrots
2	cups water
1	medium onion, chopped
1/2	cup butter, *divided*
1	can (10 3/4 ounces) condensed cream of celery soup, undiluted
1/2	cup shredded cheddar cheese
1/8	teaspoon pepper
3	cups seasoned stuffing croutons

In a large saucepan, bring carrots and water to a boil. Reduce heat; cover and simmer for 5-8 minutes or until tender. Drain. In a small skillet, saute onion in 3 tablespoons butter until tender.

In a large bowl, combine the carrots, onion, soup, cheese and pepper. Melt remaining butter; toss with stuffing. Fold into carrot mixture.

Transfer to a greased shallow 2-qt. baking dish. Cover and bake at 350° for 20 minutes. Uncover; bake 10 minutes longer or until lightly browned.

YIELD: 6 servings.

CALICO SQUASH CASSEROLE

LUCILLE TERRY, FRANKFORT, KENTUCKY

PREP: 20 min. BAKE: 30 min.

- 2 cups sliced yellow summer squash (¼ inch thick)
- 1 cup sliced zucchini (¼ inch thick)
- 1 medium onion, chopped
- ¼ cup sliced green onions
- 1 cup water
- 1 teaspoon salt, *divided*
- 2 cups crushed butter-flavored crackers
- ½ cup butter, melted
- 1 can (10 ¾ ounces) condensed cream of chicken soup, undiluted
- 1 can (8 ounces) sliced water chestnuts, drained
- 1 large carrot, shredded
- ½ cup mayonnaise
- 1 jar (2 ounces) diced pimientos, drained
- 1 teaspoon rubbed sage
- ½ teaspoon white pepper
- 1 cup (4 ounces) shredded sharp cheddar cheese

In a saucepan, combine the squash, onions, water and ½ teaspoon salt. Bring to a boil. Reduce heat; cover and cook until for 6 minutes or until squash is tender. Drain well; set aside.

Combine crumbs and butter; spoon half into a greased shallow 1½-qt. baking dish. Combine the soup, water chestnuts, carrot, mayonnaise, pimientos, sage, pepper and remaining salt; fold into squash mixture. Spoon over crumbs. Sprinkle with cheese and the remaining crumb mixture. Bake, uncovered, at 350° for 30 minutes or until lightly browned.

YIELD: 8 servings.

EDITOR'S NOTE: Reduced-fat or fat-free mayonnaise is not recommended for this recipe.

MUSHROOM CORN BREAD DRESSING

RUBY WILLIAMS, BOGALUSA, LOUISIANA

PREP: 20 min. BAKE: 65 min.

- 2 cups cornmeal
- 3 teaspoons sugar
- 3 teaspoons baking powder
- 1 teaspoon salt
- 5 eggs
- 1 can (12 ounces) evaporated milk
- ¼ cup vegetable oil
- 2 cups chopped fresh mushrooms
- 1 cup chopped celery
- ½ cup chopped green onions
- 3 tablespoons butter
- 2 cans (14½ ounces *each*) chicken broth
- 1 can (10 ¾ ounces) condensed cream of chicken soup, undiluted
- ¼ cup sliced almonds, toasted
- 1 teaspoon poultry seasoning
- ¼ teaspoon pepper

For corn bread, in a bowl, combine the cornmeal, sugar, baking powder and salt. Combine 2 eggs, milk and oil; stir into dry ingredients just until moistened. Pour into a greased 9-in. square baking pan. Bake at 400° for 18-20 minutes or until a toothpick comes out clean. Cool on a wire rack.

In a skillet, saute the mushrooms, celery and onions in butter until tender. In a large bowl, beat remaining eggs. Add the broth, soup, almonds, poultry seasoning, pepper and vegetables. Crumble corn bread over mixture.

Pour into a greased 13-in. x 9-in. x 2-in. baking dish. Bake, uncovered, at 350° for 45-50 minutes or until a knife comes out clean. Let stand for 5 minutes before cutting.

YIELD: 10-12 servings.

FLORET NOODLE BAKE

TARA BRICCO, COVINGTON, TENNESSEE

PREP: 20 min. **BAKE:** 30 min.

- 8 ounces wide egg noodles
- 1 can (10 3/4 ounces) condensed cream of mushroom soup, undiluted
- 1 cup (8 ounces) sour cream
- 3/4 cup chopped onion
- 1 teaspoon salt
- 1/4 teaspoon pepper
- 1 package (10 ounces) frozen chopped broccoli, thawed
- 1 package (8 ounces) frozen cauliflower, thawed and cut into bite-size pieces
- 1 1/2 cups (6 ounces) shredded Swiss cheese, *divided*

Cook noodles according to package directions; drain. In a large bowl, combine the soup, sour cream, onion, salt and pepper. Add the broccoli, cauliflower, noodles and 1/4 cup cheese; mix gently.

Pour into a greased 13-in. x 9-in. x 2-in. baking dish. Top with remaining cheese. Bake, uncovered, at 350° for 30 minutes or until heated through.

YIELD: 6-8 servings.

BEANS WITH CELERY BACON SAUCE

CHRISTINE EILERTS, TULSA, OKLAHOMA

PREP/TOTAL TIME: 20 min.

6	cups fresh green beans
4	bacon strips, diced
1	cup finely chopped onion
1	can (10 ¾ ounces) condensed cream of celery soup, undiluted
½	cup milk

Place beans in a large saucepan and cover with water; bring to a boil. Cook, uncovered, for 8-10 minutes or until crisp-tender; drain and set aside.

In a skillet, cook bacon over medium heat until crisp. Using a slotted spoon, remove to paper towels; drain, reserving 2 tablespoons drippings. Saute onion in drippings until tender. Stir in soup and milk until blended; heat through. Spoon over beans. Sprinkle bacon over top.

YIELD: 8 servings.

COOKING  TIP

You'll need to purchase about 2 pounds of fresh beans to equal 6 cups of cut green beans.

HEARTY VEGETABLE CASSEROLE

BILL COWAN, HANOVER, ONTARIO

PREP: 15 min. **BAKE:** 1½ hours

- 1 package (12 ounces) fresh pork sausage links
- 1 cup sliced turnips
- 1 cup diced carrots
- 1 cup diced potatoes
- 1 cup frozen peas
- 1 cup diced parsnips
- 1 cup shredded cabbage
  Salt and pepper to taste
- 1 can (8 ounces) cut green beans
- 2 tablespoons chopped onion
- 1 can (10¾ ounces) condensed cream of mushroom soup, undiluted

In a large skillet, cook sausage over medium heat until no longer pink. Meanwhile, in a greased 13-in. x 9-in. x 2-in. baking dish, layer the turnips, carrots, potatoes, peas, parsnips and cabbage, seasoning with salt and pepper between layers. Drain beans, reserving liquid. Place beans over cabbage; sprinkle with salt and pepper. Top with onion.

Drain sausage and place over onion. Combine soup and bean liquid; pour over sausage. Cover and bake at 350° for 1 hour. Uncover; turn sausage over. Bake 30 minutes longer or until vegetables are tender.

YIELD: 6 servings.

GOLDEN AU GRATIN POTATOES

LAVONNE HARTEL, WILLISTON, NORTH DAKOTA

PREP: 10 min. **BAKE:** 50 min.

- 1 can (10¾ ounces) condensed cream of chicken soup, undiluted
- 1 cup (8 ounces) sour cream
- ¾ cup butter, melted, *divided*
- 3 tablespoons dried minced onion
- ½ teaspoon salt
- 1 package (32 ounces) frozen Southern-style hash brown potatoes, thawed
- 2½ cups shredded cheddar cheese
- 2½ cups crushed cornflakes

In a large bowl, combine the soup, sour cream, ½ cup butter, onion and salt. Stir in potatoes and cheese.

Transfer to a greased 13-in. x 9-in. x 2-in. baking dish. Toss cornflakes and remaining butter; sprinkle over potatoes. Bake, uncovered, at 350° for 50-60 minutes or until heated through.

YIELD: 8-10 servings.

In a medium skillet, saute the celery, onion and red pepper in 2 tablespoons butter for 2-3 minutes or until vegetables are tender. Remove from the heat; stir in the soup, corn, water chestnuts and almonds if desired.

Transfer to a greased shallow 2-qt. baking dish. Melt remaining butter; toss with bread crumbs. Sprinkle on top. Bake, uncovered, at 350° for 25-30 minutes or until bubbly.

YIELD: 8 servings.

WILD RICE STUFFING BAKE

FRANCES POSTE, WALL, SOUTH DAKOTA

PREP: 25 min. **BAKE:** 30 min.

$1/2$	cup chopped celery
$1/3$	cup chopped onion
3	tablespoons butter
1	egg
1	can (10 $3/4$ ounces) condensed cream of chicken soup, undiluted
$1/2$	cup chicken broth
1	tablespoon minced fresh parsley
$1/2$	teaspoon poultry seasoning
$1/4$	teaspoon salt
$1/8$	teaspoon pepper
3	cups day-old bread cubes
$1 1/2$	cups cooked wild rice

In a skillet, saute celery and onion in butter until tender. Combine the egg, soup, broth, parsley, poultry seasoning, salt and pepper. Add celery mixture, bread cubes and rice; mix well.

Spoon into a greased shallow 1 $1/2$-qt. baking dish. Cover and bake at 350° for 20 minutes. Uncover; bake 10-15 minutes longer or until set.

YIELD: 6-8 servings.

CREAMY CORN CASSEROLE

BRENDA WOOD, EGBERT, ONTARIO

PREP: 15 min. **BAKE:** 25 min.

1	cup finely chopped celery
$1/4$	cup finely chopped onion
$1/4$	cup finely chopped sweet red pepper
3	tablespoons butter, *divided*
1	can (10 $3/4$ ounces) condensed cream of chicken soup, undiluted
3	cups fresh, frozen *or* drained canned corn
1	can (8 ounces) sliced water chestnuts, drained
$1/3$	cup slivered almonds, optional
$1/2$	cup soft bread crumbs

SWISS ONIONS

BETH PERRY, JACKSONVILLE, FLORIDA

PREP: 15 min. **BAKE:** 30 min.

- 3   large sweet onions, sliced
- 2   tablespoons butter
- 2   cups (8 ounces) shredded Swiss cheese, *divided*
-     Pepper to taste
- 1   can (10 ¾ ounces) condensed cream of chicken soup, undiluted
- ⅔   cup milk
- 1   teaspoon soy sauce
- 8   slices French bread, buttered on both sides

In a large skillet, saute onions in butter. Layer onions and two-thirds of the cheese in a greased shallow 2-qt. baking dish, sprinkling pepper between layers.

In a saucepan, heat the soup, milk and soy sauce; stir to blend. Pour over onions and stir gently. Top with bread. Bake, uncovered, at 350° for 15 minutes. Push bread under sauce; sprinkle with remaining cheese. Bake 15 minutes longer or until heated through.

YIELD: 8 servings.

CROUTON CELERY CASSEROLE

ELIZABETH PARKE, FORT WAYNE, INDIANA

PREP/TOTAL TIME: 30 min.

- 4 cups thinly sliced celery
- 1 can (10 3/4 ounces) condensed cream of celery *or* chicken soup, undiluted
- 1 can (8 ounces) sliced water chestnuts, drained and halved
- 1 1/4 cups seasoned salad croutons, *divided*
- 1/2 cup plus 2 tablespoons slivered almonds, *divided*
- 1 tablespoon butter, melted

Place celery in a saucepan and cover with water. Cover and bring to a boil. Reduce heat; cook, uncovered, for 5-6 minutes or until crisp-tender. Drain and place in a bowl. Add the soup, water chestnuts, 1 cup croutons and 1/2 cup almonds. Transfer to a greased shallow 1 1/2-qt. baking dish.

Crush remaining croutons; toss with butter and remaining almonds. Sprinkle over the top. Bake, uncovered, at 350° for 20-25 minutes or until heated through and top is golden brown.

YIELD: 6-8 servings.

SAUSAGE PILAF

KELLY MORRISSEY, OVERLAND PARK, KANSAS

PREP: 15 min. **BAKE:** 1 hour 10 min.

- 1/2 pound bulk pork sausage
- 1 cup chopped celery
- 1/2 cup chopped onion
- 1/2 cup chopped green pepper
- 1 can (10 3/4 ounces) condensed cream of mushroom soup, undiluted
- 1 1/4 cups milk
- 1 jar (2 ounces) diced pimientos, drained
- 1/2 cup uncooked long grain rice
- 1/2 teaspoon poultry seasoning
- 1/4 teaspoon salt
- 1 cup soft bread crumbs
- 2 tablespoons butter, melted

In a skillet, cook the sausage, celery, onion and green pepper over medium heat until sausage is no longer pink and vegetables are tender; drain. Stir in the soup, milk, pimientos, rice, poultry seasoning and salt.

Pour into an ungreased 1 1/2-qt. baking dish. Cover and bake at 350° for 50 minutes, stirring occasionally.

Combine bread crumbs and butter; sprinkle on top. Bake, uncovered, 20 minutes more.

YIELD: 6-8 servings.

BROCCOLI SUPREME

LUCY PARKS, BIRMINGHAM, ALABAMA

PREP: 10 min. **BAKE:** 50 min.

- 2 tablespoons all-purpose flour
- 2 cans (10 3/4 ounces *each*) condensed cream of chicken soup, undiluted
- 1 cup (8 ounces) sour cream
- 1/2 cup grated carrot
- 2 tablespoons grated onion
- 1/2 teaspoon pepper
- 3 packages (10 ounces *each*) frozen broccoli cuts, thawed
- 1 1/2 cups crushed seasoned stuffing
- 1/4 cup butter, melted

In a large bowl, combine the flour, soup and sour cream. Stir in the carrot, onion and pepper. Fold in the broccoli.

Transfer to a greased shallow 2 1/2-qt. baking dish. Combine stuffing and butter; sprinkle over top. Bake, uncovered, at 350° for 50-60 minutes or until bubbly and heated through.

YIELD: 12 servings.

SQUASH BAKE

THELMA MEFFORD, WETUMKA, OKLAHOMA

PREP: 20 min. **BAKE:** 25 min.

- 8 cups sliced yellow squash (about 2 pounds)
- 1/2 cup chopped onion
- 3/4 cup shredded carrots
- 1/4 cup butter
- 1 can (10 3/4 ounces) condensed cream of chicken soup, undiluted
- 1/2 cup sour cream
- 2 cups herb stuffing croutons, *divided*

In a large saucepan; bring 2 in. water and squash to a boil. Reduce heat; cook for 3 to 4 minutes or until crisp-tender. Drain well.

In a skillet, saute onion and carrots in butter until tender. Combine onion and carrots with the soup, sour cream and 1 1/2 cups croutons. Add squash and mix lightly.

Spoon into a lightly greased 11-in. x 7-in. x 2-in. or shallow 2-qt. baking dish. Sprinkle with the remaining croutons. Bake, uncovered, at 350° for 25 minutes or until heated through.

YIELD: 8-10 servings.

Toss the cornflakes and butter; sprinkle half into a greased 13-in. x 9-in. x 2-in. baking dish. Layer with the cabbage, onion, salt and pepper.

In a bowl, combine the soup, milk and mayonnaise until smooth. Spoon over top; sprinkle with cheese and remaining cornflake mixture. Bake, uncovered, at 350° for 45-50 minutes or until golden brown.

YIELD: **8-10 servings.**

EDITOR'S NOTE: Reduced-fat or fat-free mayonnaise is not recommended for this recipe.

CRUMB-TOPPED VEGETABLE BAKE

MAXINE SIMES, SIDNEY, OHIO

PREP: 15 min. **BAKE:** 30 min.

1	package (24 ounces) frozen California-blend vegetables
1	can (10 3/4 ounces) condensed cream of celery soup, undiluted
1	jar (8 ounces) process cheese sauce
1/2	cup finely crushed butter-flavored crackers (about 13 crackers)
2	tablespoons butter, melted

Prepare vegetables according to package directions; drain. In a bowl, combine the soup and cheese sauce. Add vegetables and stir to coat.

Transfer to a greased shallow 2-qt. baking dish. Toss cracker crumbs and butter; sprinkle over the top. Bake, uncovered, at 350° for 30 minutes or until heated through.

YIELD: **6 servings.**

CHEDDAR CABBAGE CASSEROLE

ALICE JONES, DEMOREST, GEORGIA

PREP: 10 min. **BAKE:** 45 min.

2 1/2	cups coarsely crushed cornflakes
1/2	cup butter, melted
4 1/2	cups shredded cabbage
1/3	cup chopped onion
1/4	to 1/2 teaspoon salt
1/4	to 1/2 teaspoon pepper
1	can (10 3/4 ounces) condensed cream of celery soup, undiluted
1	cup milk
1/2	cup mayonnaise
2	cups (8 ounces) shredded cheddar cheese

FESTIVE PEAS AND ONIONS

CARAMELLA ROBICHAUD, RICHIBUCTO, NEW BRUNSWICK

PREP: 35 min. **BAKE:** 40 min.

- 1 package (16 ounces) frozen pearl onions
- 2 cups water
- 1 package (10 ounces) frozen peas, thawed
- 1 can (10 3/4 ounces) condensed cream of celery soup, undiluted
- 1 jar (2 ounces) diced pimientos, *divided*
- 1/3 cup shredded sharp cheddar cheese

In a saucepan, bring onions in water to a boil. Reduce heat; cover and cook for 25 minutes or until tender. Drain, reserving 1/4 cup liquid.

Combine the onions, peas, soup, 2 tablespoons pimientos and reserved cooking liquid; stir to coat. Transfer to a greased shallow 1 1/2-qt. baking dish.

Bake, uncovered, at 350° for 35 minutes. Sprinkle with cheese and remaining pimientos. Bake 5 minutes longer or until the cheese is melted.

YIELD: 4-6 servings.

SAUCY POTATOES

EDNA HOFFMAN, HEBRON, INDIANA

PREP/TOTAL TIME: 15 min.

- 1 can (10 3/4 ounces) condensed cream of chicken soup, undiluted
- 1/4 cup chicken broth
- 5 medium potatoes, peeled, cooked and cubed

In a saucepan, combine soup and broth; stir in potatoes. Cook over medium-low heat until mixture just begins to simmer and potatoes are heated through.

YIELD: 4 servings.

SPECIAL BRUSSELS SPROUTS

RUBY MIGUEZ, CROWLEY, LOUISIANA

PREP/TOTAL TIME: 15 min.

1/4	cup sliced almonds
1	tablespoon butter
1	package (16 ounces) frozen brussels sprouts
1	chicken bouillon cube
1	can (10 3/4 ounces) condensed cream of chicken soup, undiluted
2	tablespoons milk
1	jar (2 ounces) chopped pimientos, drained
1/4	teaspoon pepper
1/8	teaspoon dried thyme

In a small skillet, saute almonds in butter until lightly browned; set aside. In a saucepan, cook brussels sprouts according to package directions, adding the bouillon cube to the water.

Meanwhile, in another saucepan, combine the soup, milk, pimientos, pepper and thyme. Cook until heated through. Drain sprouts; top with the cream sauce and stir gently. Sprinkle with almonds.

YIELD: 4-6 servings.

COOKING TIP

Instead of almonds, use toasted pecans to add a buttery, nutty flavor to the brussels sprouts.

RANCH POTATOES

ELAINE EAVENSON, MOSELLE, MASSACHUSETTS

PREP: 20 min. **BAKE:** 25 min.

8	to 10 medium potatoes, peeled and cut into ¹/₂-inch cubes
1	can (10 ³/₄ ounces) condensed cream of mushroom soup, undiluted
1¹/₄	cups milk
1	envelope ranch salad dressing mix
1¹/₄	cups shredded sharp cheddar cheese, *divided*
	Salt and pepper to taste
6	bacon strips, cooked and crumbled

Place potatoes in a saucepan and cover with water. Bring to a boil. Reduce heat; cover and cook for 10 minutes or until almost tender. Drain; place in a greased 13-in. x 9-in. x 2-in. baking dish.

Combine the soup, milk, salad dressing mix, 1 cup cheese, salt and pepper; pour over potatoes. Top with bacon and remaining cheese. Bake, uncovered, at 350° for 25-30 minutes or until potatoes are tender.

YIELD: 10 servings.

CARROTS SUPREME

LISE THOMSON, MAGRATH, ALBERTA

PREP: 15 min. **BAKE:** 30 min.

8	cups sliced carrots
1	small onion, chopped
1	tablespoon butter
1	can (10 ³/₄ ounces) condensed cream of mushroom soup, undiluted
1	can (4 ounces) mushroom stems and pieces, drained
¹/₂	cup grated Parmesan cheese
1	cup soft bread crumbs

Place 2 in. of water in a large saucepan; add carrots. Bring to a boil. Reduce heat; cover and simmer for 7-9 minutes or until crisp-tender. Meanwhile, in a small skillet, saute onion in butter until tender. Drain carrots; add onion, soup, mushrooms and Parmesan cheese.

Transfer to a greased shallow 2¹/₂-qt. baking dish. Sprinkle with bread crumbs. Bake, uncovered, at 350° for 30-35 minutes or until heated through.

YIELD: 8 servings.

GREEN BEAN POTATO BAKE

CHARLENE WELLS, COLORADO SPRINGS, COLORADO

PREP: 10 min. **BAKE:** 50 min.

6	cups cubed peeled cooked potatoes
2	cups frozen cut green beans, thawed
2	cups cubed fully cooked ham
2 1/2	cups (10 ounces) shredded Colby-Monterey Jack cheese, *divided*
2	tablespoons dried minced onion
1	can (10 3/4 ounces) condensed cream of mushroom soup, undiluted
1/2	cup milk
1/3	cup mayonnaise
1/3	cup sour cream

In a greased 13-in. x 9-in. x 2-in. baking dish, layer the potatoes, beans, ham, 2 cups cheese and onion. In a bowl, combine the soup, milk, mayonnaise and sour cream; pour over the top and gently stir to coat.

Cover and bake at 350° for 45 minutes. Uncover; sprinkle with remaining cheese. Bake 5-8 minutes longer or until cheese is melted.

YIELD: 8 servings.

EDITOR'S NOTE: Reduced-fat or fat-free mayonnaise is not recommended for this recipe.

CREAMY PEA CASSEROLE

MARY PAULINE MAYNOR, FRANKLINTON, LOUISIANA

PREP: 15 min. **BAKE:** 25 min.

- 1 medium onion, chopped
- 3 celery ribs, finely chopped
- 1/2 medium sweet red pepper
- 6 tablespoons butter
- 1 can (10 3/4 ounces) condensed cream of mushroom soup, undiluted
- 1 tablespoon milk
- 2 cups frozen peas, thawed
- 1 can (8 ounces) sliced water chestnuts, drained
- 1/2 to 3/4 cup crushed butter-flavored crackers (about 12 crackers)

In a skillet, saute the onion, celery and red pepper in butter for 8-10 minutes or until tender. Stir in soup and milk; heat through. Stir in peas and water chestnuts.

Transfer to a greased shallow 1 1/2-qt. baking dish. Sprinkle with the cracker crumbs. Bake, uncovered, at 350° for 25-30 minutes or until bubbly.

YIELD: 6 servings.

COOKING TIP

When you make Creamy Pea Casserole, you'll have a half of a sweet red pepper left over. Simply chop or slice the leftover pepper and place in a small freezer bag. It can be kept in the freezer for 8 to 12 months.

HUNGARIAN NOODLE SIDE DISH

BETTY SUGG, AKRON, NEW YORK

PREP: 15 min. **BAKE:** 45 min.

- 1 package (16 ounces) medium noodles
- 3 chicken bouillon cubes
- 1/4 cup boiling water
- 1 can (10 3/4 ounces) condensed cream of mushroom soup, undiluted
- 1/2 cup chopped onion
- 2 tablespoons Worcestershire sauce
- 2 tablespoons poppy seeds
- 1/8 to 1/4 teaspoon garlic powder
- 1/8 to 1/4 teaspoon hot pepper sauce
- 2 cups (16 ounces) cottage cheese
- 2 cups (16 ounces) sour cream
- 1/4 cup shredded Parmesan cheese
  Paprika

Cook noodles according to package directions. Meanwhile, in a large bowl, dissolve bouillon in water. Add the soup, onion, Worcestershire sauce, poppy seeds, garlic powder and hot pepper sauce; mix well. Stir in the cottage cheese, sour cream and noodles and mix well.

Pour into a greased shallow 2 1/2-qt. baking dish. Sprinkle with the Parmesan cheese and paprika. Cover and bake at 350° for 45 minutes or until heated through.

YIELD: 8-10 servings.

BROCCOLI WITH RICE

SONDRA OSTHEIMER, BOSCOBEL, WISCONSIN

PREP/TOTAL TIME: 20 min.

1	package (16 ounces) frozen broccoli cuts
1½	cups cooked rice
1	can (10 ¾ ounces) condensed cream of mushroom soup, undiluted

In a saucepan, cook broccoli according to package directions; drain. Add rice and soup. Cook until heated through.

YIELD: 4 servings.

CHEESY CARROTS

LOIS HARBOLD, ELIZABETHTOWN, PENNSYLVANIA

PREP/TOTAL TIME: 30 min.

1	package (16 ounces) frozen sliced carrots, thawed
1	can (10 ¾ ounces) condensed cream of celery soup, undiluted
8	ounces process cheese (Velveeta), cubed

⅓	cup dry bread crumbs
2	tablespoons butter, melted

In a bowl, combine the carrots, soup and cheese. Transfer to a greased shallow 1½-qt. baking dish. Bake, uncovered, at 350° for 10 minutes; stir. Toss bread crumbs and butter; sprinkle over top. Bake 10-15 minutes longer or until carrots are tender and mixture is bubbly.

YIELD: 4-6 servings.

CHEDDAR TATERS

RUTH VAN NATTAN, KINGSTON, TENNESSEE

PREP: 5 min. **BAKE:** 30 min.

1	can (10 ¾ ounces) condensed cream of chicken soup, undiluted
1	can (12 ounces) evaporated milk
1	cup (8 ounces) sour cream
½	cup butter, melted
1	teaspoon garlic powder
1	teaspoon onion powder
1	package (32 ounces) frozen Tater Tots
1½	cups (6 ounces) shredded cheddar cheese
1	cup crushed potato chips

In a large bowl, combine the soup, milk, sour cream, butter and seasonings. Gently stir in the Tater Tots.

Transfer to a greased 13-in. x 9-in. x 2-in. baking dish. Sprinkle with cheese and potato chips. Bake, uncovered, at 350° for 30-35 minutes or until bubbly.

YIELD: 8-10 servings.

CREAMY POTATO STICKS

MARIE HOYER, HODGENVILLE, KENTUCKY

PREP: 15 min. **BAKE:** 55 min.

- 1/4   cup all-purpose flour
- 1/2   teaspoon salt
- 1 1/2 cups milk
- 1   can (10 3/4 ounces) condensed cream of celery soup, undiluted
- 1/2   pound process cheese (Velveeta), cubed
- 5   to 6 large baking potatoes, peeled
- 1   cup chopped onion
         Paprika

In a saucepan, combine flour and salt; gradually whisk in milk until smooth. Bring to a boil; cook and stir for 2 minutes. Remove from the heat; whisk in soup and cheese until smooth. Set aside.

Cut potatoes into 4-in. x 1/2-in. x 1/2-in. sticks; place in a greased 13-in. x 9-in. x 2-in. baking dish. Sprinkle with onion. Top with cheese sauce.

Bake, uncovered, at 350° for 55-60 minutes or until potatoes are tender. Sprinkle with paprika.

YIELD: 6 servings.

VEGETABLE NOODLE CASSEROLE

JEANETTE HIOS, BROOKLYN, NEW YORK

PREP: 15 min. **BAKE:** 45 min.

1	package (16 ounces) wide egg noodles
1	can (10 ¾ ounces) condensed cream of chicken soup, undiluted
1	can (10 ¾ ounces) condensed cream of broccoli soup, undiluted
1½	cups milk
1	cup grated Parmesan cheese, *divided*
3	garlic cloves, minced
2	tablespoons dried parsley flakes
½	teaspoon pepper
¼	teaspoon salt
1	package (16 ounces) frozen California-blend vegetables, thawed
2	cup frozen corn, thawed

Cook noodles according to package directions. In a bowl, combine the soups, milk, ¾ cup Parmesan cheese, garlic, parsley, pepper and salt. Drain noodles and add to soup mixture along with the vegetables; mix well.

Pour into a greased 13-in. x 9-in. x 2-in. baking dish. Sprinkle with the remaining Parmesan. Cover and bake at 350° for 45-50 minutes or until heated through.

YIELD: 12-14 servings.

FANCY BEAN CASSEROLE

VENOLA SHARPE, CAMPBELLSVILLE, KENTUCKY

PREP: 15 min. **BAKE:** 40 min.

3	cups frozen French-style green beans
1	can (10 ¾ ounces) condensed cream of chicken soup, undiluted
1	can (11 ounces) shoepeg corn, drained
1	cup (8 ounces) sour cream
1	can (8 ounces) sliced water chestnuts, drained
½	cup shredded process cheese (Velveeta)
1	medium onion, chopped
3	tablespoons butter
¾	cup crushed butter-flavored crackers (about 18 crackers)
¼	cup slivered almonds

In a large bowl, combine the first seven ingredients. Transfer to a greased shallow 2-qt. baking dish. In a skillet, melt butter. Add cracker crumbs and almonds; cook and stir until lightly browned. Sprinkle over top.

Bake, uncovered, at 350° for 40-45 minutes or until heated through and topping is golden brown.

YIELD: 6 servings.

GOLDEN BAKED ONIONS

CHRIS GASKILL, KNOXVILLE, TENNESSEE

PREP: 20 min. **BAKE:** 25 min.

6	large sweet onions, thinly sliced
1/4	cup butter
1	can (10 3/4 ounces) condensed cream of chicken soup, undiluted
1/2	cup milk
1/8	teaspoon pepper
3	cups (12 ounces) shredded Swiss cheese, *divided*
6	slices French bread (3/4 inch thick)
2	tablespoons butter, melted

In a large skillet, saute onions in butter until tender, about 12 minutes. In a bowl, combine the soup, milk, pepper and 2 cups cheese. Stir in onions.

Transfer to a greased shallow 2-qt. baking dish. Sprinkle with remaining cheese. Brush bread slices with melted butter on one side. Arrange buttered side up over cheese.

Bake, uncovered, at 350° for 25-30 minutes or until bubbly. If desired, broil 4-6 in. from heat until bread is golden brown. Let stand for 5 minutes before serving.

YIELD: 6-8 servings.

GREEN CHILI RICE

SANDRA HANSON, EMERY, SOUTH DAKOTA

PREP/TOTAL TIME: 30 min.

1	can (10 3/4 ounces) condensed cream of celery soup, undiluted
1	cup (8 ounces) sour cream
1	can (4 ounces) green chilies
1	cup (4 ounces) shredded cheddar cheese
1 1/2	cups uncooked instant rice

In a bowl, combine the soup, sour cream, chilies and cheese. Stir in rice.

Transfer to a greased shallow 1 1/2-qt. baking dish. Bake, uncovered, at 350° for 20 minutes or until rice is tender.

YIELD: 4-6 servings.

CHEESE VEGGIE BAKE

TAMI KRATZER, WEST JORDAN, UTAH

PREP: 10 min. **BAKE:** 25 min.

- 1 package (16 ounces) frozen broccoli, carrots and cauliflower
- 1 can (10 ¾ ounces) condensed cream of mushroom soup, undiluted
- 1 carton (8 ounces) spreadable garden vegetable cream cheese
- ½ to 1 cup seasoned croutons

Prepare vegetables according to package directions; drain and place in a large bowl. Stir in soup and cream cheese.

Transfer to a greased shallow 1-qt. baking dish. Sprinkle with croutons. Bake, uncovered, at 375° for 25 minutes or until bubbly.

YIELD: 6 servings.

MUSHROOM WILD RICE

EDNA EGGERT, BELLA VISTA, ARKANSAS

PREP: 20 min. + standing BAKE: 2½ hours

3	cups boiling water
1	cup uncooked wild rice
1½	pounds ground beef
1	small onion, chopped
1	pound fresh mushrooms, halved
2	cans (10 ¾ ounces *each*) condensed cream of chicken soup, undiluted
1	can (10 ½ ounces) beef consomme
1⅓	cups water
½	cup slivered almonds
1	tablespoon minced fresh parsley
1	bay leaf
½	teaspoon salt
¼	teaspoon *each* celery salt, garlic salt and onion salt
¼	teaspoon poultry seasoning
¼	teaspoon paprika
¼	teaspoon pepper
	Pinch dried thyme

In a bowl, combine water and rice; let stand for 15 minutes. Meanwhile, in a large skillet, cook beef and onion over medium heat until the meat is no longer pink; drain. Add mushrooms; saute for 2 minutes. Stir in the remaining ingredients. Drain rice and stir into beef mixture. Remove from the heat; cool.

Transfer to a greased 13-in. x 9-in. x 2-in. baking dish. Cover and bake at 350° for 2 hours. Uncover; bake 30 minutes longer or until rice is tender. Discard bay leaf.

YIELD: 6-8 servings.

WESTERN POTATOES

JANICE THOMPSON, MARTIN, MICHIGAN

PREP: 15 min. BAKE: 25 min. + standing

½	cup chopped sweet red pepper
½	cup chopped onion
2	tablespoons butter
1	can (10 ¾ ounces) condensed cream of celery soup, undiluted
¼	cup milk
1	can (4 ounces) chopped green chilies
¼	teaspoon salt
⅛	teaspoon cayenne pepper, optional
⅛	teaspoon hot pepper sauce
1	cup (4 ounces) shredded cheddar cheese, *divided*
8	cooked medium red potatoes, cubed

In a large saucepan or Dutch oven, saute red pepper and onion in butter until tender. Stir in the soup, milk, chilies, salt, cayenne if desired and hot pepper sauce; heat through. Stir in ¾ cup cheese until melted. Add the potatoes; stir to coat.

Transfer to a greased 11-in. x 7-in. x 2-in. baking dish. Bake, uncovered, at 350° for 20-25 minutes or until bubbly. Sprinkle with remaining cheese. Bake 5 minutes longer or until cheese is melted. Let stand for 10 minutes before serving.

YIELD: 6-8 servings.

General Index

Alphabetical Index